For the love of Jesus + Mary —

Aurora

Aurora

AURORA P. STA. ANA

XULON PRESS

Xulon Press
2301 Lucien Way #415
Maitland, FL 32751
407.339.4217
www.xulonpress.com

© 2020 by Aurora P. Sta. Ana

Unless otherwise indicated, Scripture quotations taken from the Holy Bible, New International Version (NIV). Copyright © 1973, 1978, 1984, 2011 by Biblica, Inc.™. Used by permission. All rights reserved.

Printed in the United States of America.

ISBN-13: 978-1-6305-0370-3

Dedicated to Bossing, my super hero, and my five hearts;
Nique, Micci, Audrie, Lady, and Cesareo

And to all those who will benefit from the proceeds of this book.

Table of Contents

Foreword

I have known Aurora or Au, as we called her then, for a very long time. Not only did I know her personally, we were also very close. We taught in the same school in a posh village south of Manila about 20 years ago. I knew her as we were always together with our common friends practically every day during those years. Even more so, I saw the love blossoming between her and her then husband to-be. Hence, I knew her like the palm of my hand, or so I thought. That was until I got to read her book. What a revelation it was! None of those written in this book were known to me nor to her closest friends in school. Nobody knew. She kept everything from us and neither anybody knew nor will ever know why people are just different from each other, I guess. Had I known what I have discovered reading her life story, I would not have hesitated to extend help to her had she asked for it. The things she had to endure were so intense that anybody with a faint heart would have given up a long time ago.

From the day she was born, Au had been living a life of discomfort. To make a difficult existence even worse, one by one, the hurdles she had to overcome became harder—the cross she carried got heavier by the years, just waiting for her to be nailed on it. Using a deck of cards as an analogy, she was dealt a shitty hand of cards. Worse, she was thrown several curve balls to boot, enough to make her life miserable by any ordinary individual's standards. However, she was far from ordinary. Armed with a brain she learned to nurture with beautiful thoughts, developed the perseverance to study hard and hone her intellectual skills, coupled with a strong resolve and wily wit to beat the odds, she survived them all. She knew how to play the bad hands she had been dealt with, managed to stay afloat and even won in the end.

While on the surface, this book is about Au and her travails in life, one has to read it on different levels. First and foremost, it tells us how to live poor in an already poor country. Being bad enough to live in a land full of wants; to live in utter deprivation in such a horrid place is unthinkable. Second, through this book, one gets a glimpse of the Filipino culture and how Filipinos thrive in spite of having to eke out a living. In a land where there is a great divide between the haves and have-nots, it is impossible to see how different one's world is from those with plenty and view life with a lot of envy. Not my Au though. She was content with what she had and grew up not wanting what she cannot have—material things that is. Third, the reader will know that one of the distinct characteristics of a Filipino is to learn how to look at life with humor. Dubbed as one of the happiest people on earth, Filipinos have learned to laugh at themselves and their misfortunes. This feature is very evident in Au's writing as she narrates how poor her family was, yet she injected humor in the narrative giving away how she managed to look at life. Lastly, being religious, a believer of the Catholic faith and devoted to the Virgin Mother, she had surrendered everything to the Lord, but unlike the fanatic, she does so only after having done what she thought she had to do. These levels are manifested either explicitly or implicitly throughout the pages in this book.

It has been said that we can only truly appreciate the blessings in our lives after we have suffered and worked hard for them. We tend to ignore the pleasures and benefits of life when these are given to us on a silver platter. Au has had one misfortune after another throughout her life, and she had avowed that all sacrifices and everything she did were all for the love of her Creator. Luckily, her tables have turned, and she now reaps the benefits after a long, arduous life of misery. That is my only consolation after having read her life story—it seems that the trials in her life are now over. It is now time to reap the right to enjoy the remaining years of her life, hopefully, for a very long time—even a lot longer than the years of her suffering. Let this book be an inspiration to everyone knowing that no matter how dark the tunnel of life may be, it has to end somewhere, and at the end is an illuminating light, radiant and bright enough to guide our paths with clarity no matter how long the journey shall be.

Rolly S. delos Santos

Prologue

I love telling stories and sharing my childhood experiences to my children and friends. I do this not because I want them to be sorry for me, but because I want to impart what I learned from my sad experiences. I find that people in this day and age, especially the teenagers and young adults, give up easily when faced with adversity and confronted with conflicts in their professional, personal, and social lives. I feel the need to share what I went through and how I got through it. I know there are people who have worse problems than me, but I want others to know the impactful role my faith has played in solving my life's issues. Making good choices and just believing will go a long way. The people who have heard bits and pieces of my story have said that I have an inspiring life. I would agree, I think. They suggested that I write a book, but I pushed that thought aside for years because I had only thought of myself as a storyteller, not a writer. As I make new friends, they all still say the same thing: **"Write a book."**

Every year, all parishioners are asked to renew their commitment to stewardship of time, talent, and treasure. We pledge what is within our means because resources are very limited for a big family like ours.

I have always wanted to do more to support our church's projects, but how? With five children in five different schools and a teacher's salary, what was there to give? Since I don't have much treasure, I try to give my time and talent by volunteering to teach grade school-level Faith Formation classes and Children's Liturgy for Grades 1-3 at our parish. In addition, my husband and I help clean or set things up at church when we get the chance. But I don't do much outside of that. My children, who are now old enough to take on responsibilities within other church ministries, help in any way they can. They have been Altar Servers, have painted the Teen Lounge room (a room at church specifically designed for teens to meet and hang out), have assembled furniture, have participated actively in the Life Teen Faith Formation classes (high school religious education group), and have accepted invitations to share a witnessing of their faith during retreats, parent's orientations, and for promoting Life Teen's fundraising events. But I don't think that's enough; our church needs more than our stewardship of talents and time. It also needs some monetary contribution to carry out other ministries.

On another note, as my children grew up and maybe heard some stories about their friends' family drama, they started to ask about my relationship with their father. I explained it to the first child, then to the second... and... I will do this again to the third, fourth and fifth? I will sound like a broken record.

Huh! That's what happens when you have too many children.

There must be a way to make this process a lot easier, I thought.

I wish I had recorded my explanation when I did it the first time, but my voice sounded weird and even now I still can't get rid of my thick Filipino accent. But I always jot down notes mostly about everything and anything funny, memorable, heart-wrenching, or even embarrassing moments that happened in my family. We cry, laugh, insult, mock, praise, work with, pray for, and love each other. We do everything together and with each other, we are a great team! People who don't know us get shocked when they hear us mock each other, but that is just our way of endearment. One time, I had the chance to look at all my notes and realized, *Hey! These will make a good book!*

As part of my bucket list, I wanted to do something worthwhile that is separate from raising five children and teaching. I am 50 years old now, and who knows how much time is left for me? My thought is, since God gave me this life, why don't I use it to raise funds for churches and schools here in the US and in the Philippines? I don't have a lot of money to share, but I have a treasure of experiences to write about. Taking into consideration all that was in my head, I figured that writing a book, like what many people told me to do, is not a bad idea after all. It will cover all the things that I wanted to do. With this, my children will get answers to all their questions, get a glimpse of my sad experiences, hopefully pick up a few lessons on how I fought my own battles, and maybe figure out how I got to be where I am right now. Also, this book wishes to share my hard-learned life's lessons to other people while supporting the parish that has become the backbone of our family.

My recent *Aha* moment: *Writing my life story when I turn 50 is something worthwhile.* I think I can do it. Initially, I thought that it was out of reach, but here it is... becoming a reality with God's love and your support. I hope you feel God as I open my life to you through the pages of this book.

God bless, and may the love of Mary live within us always!

- Aurora

1
CHAPTER

What I Remember

My earliest memory is a small house with multiple extended rooms. My parents owned the house, but the government owned the land. We occupied the "biggest" room, which was our privilege as the owners. When I say the "biggest room," I mean it was the most *decent* room. It had a sink and some electrical outlets. But my definition of "big" here might not be the same as yours. It is most likely the size of your garage or tool shed. We knew that the government could shoo us away at their discretion, but until then, my parents used our shelter as a way to make money. There were three other rooms around ours which we leased, and these rooms sourced their power from where we lived. The rent depends on convenience—you can either choose a walk-in room with electricity (you walk like a normal person in your tiny space) or a crawl-in room with no electricity at all.

What? You mean crawling in the room? What was that?

I know you are imagining what it is like to slither like a snake around in the dark.

How did they change or put some clothes on?

Oh, they sit, then they put their pants on.

Do you also have a "crawl space" in your house? Because that's what this is! A crawl space for rent.

For all the occupants, there was only one detached bathroom and one faucet outside the house; there was no running water inside the shelter. Adjacent to our house was my auntie's place. Her house had more rooms available for tenants, had a power line in all "standing" rooms, and one waterline inside the house. An indoor bathroom was also available for everybody. The tenants would line up or talk amongst themselves to determine who should get water or who could use the bathroom first. This was unlike our house, where you had to bring water in your room from the outside. I hope you get a clear picture of it.

Well, my mother appreciated any extra money that she could make from that tiny house. We are a family of five; my *Mamang* (mother), *Papang* (father), *Ate* (older sister), *Kuya* (older brother), and myself. My mother, God bless her heart, is the most hardworking person I know. She used to work seven days a week, 14 hours a day. God gave her a healthy body because she couldn't afford to be sick or miss a work day. She and her sewing machine were best buddies. She used to sew short pants and rags and got paid by the dozen. I remember her getting up from her chair only when she needed a restroom break. My father was a security guard at Armor's Food Factory, and he would sometimes bring home some rejected hotdogs and hams. From what I recall, they were sold to him at a very cheap price.

My sister, being the oldest of the three and was about 10 years old at the time, did all the household chores. She would do our laundry (hand-washed with bar soap), cook rice for us, and do errands on the side. Tidying up the house, I mean the *room*, was not really a difficult task because there wasn't much to tidy up anyway. My brother, who was about eight years old then, was always on the street with his friends. They would walk up to the landfill to collect some foil and other "valuable" trash, i.e. anything that he could sell or trade at the junk shop like metal, iron, or steel. Sometimes, he would offer to help carry a casket. Yes, with a dead man in it, for a minimal fee.

Meanwhile, I was about six years old when I started my door-to-door business. Some were blessed to own a fancy polisher, but not in my world. So I walked around with my buddy, the *bunot,* or coconut husk, offering my services as a floor polisher. I would wax other people's floor and then scrub it with *bunot* and get paid. One peso (a little less than a penny) was just enough to get myself a piece of candy. Also, whenever we got the chance, my siblings and I collected empty glass bottles and sold them to a peddler. We did everything we could to earn money.

Our elementary school was just two blocks away. Overall, we lived a pretty decent life. We had a TV, which my father bought for 50 pesos (about $1.00), so we could watch the fight of Mohammad Ali against Joe Frazier in Manila, Philippines. It was funny, though, because we couldn't cough or walk because if someone did, the TV will go off. Typical Filipino in a third world country, right? If you want to watch the entire fight, you would have to be really still—you can't even fart! If you do, the sound vibration might stir the wires inside that drawer-sized box TV.

At school, I remember being a leader. My teachers would always ask me to help them grade papers, teach my classmates their ABCs, and water all the plants, especially the hanging plants because I was one of the tallest kids in my class. I also helped them sell their goodies. In public schools, it was common for teachers to make their own treats like *yema* (milk candies) and *pastillas* (milk sticks) or repack cheese curls to sell to the students. You get plus points, and teachers will like you more if you buy their goodies.

Well... hey!

We are talking about making ends meet here. Please don't judge. Teachers needed extra income too, so they used their classrooms to add a little to their salary. To be clear, this was during my time. I'm sure there have been a lot of changes in our public school system since 1975.

I also remember always receiving free bread from the government every day. Each student got one, and of course, I used it to my advantage. What I did was, I first asked the tenants and the other people in our little community if they liked the *Nutribun,* or nutritious bun. Then, I would ask my classmates and friends if they wished to make money out of their "daily bread." My plan was to collect theirs and go back home to deliver "orders" every morning. The customers would pay me 25 centavos per bread (like a quarter of a penny, if there is such a thing). Everybody needed some extra income, so those whose bread I helped sell got 20 centavos, while I kept the remaining 5 as my walking/selling/advertising fee. That way, I earned 25 centavos from my own bread, and 5 more for every *Nutribun* that I ended up selling. So if I sold 15 buns for 25 each, I earned 75 centavos, and that meant more candies for me! I didn't care if I missed my morning classes. Yup! I ran this business during class hours. In my head I thought, *"It is okay. I can do extra work when I get back. At least, I have more than one candy!"*

Honestly, I don't remember learning a lot in the classroom. But I learned a lot in the streets because I met and talked to older people at a young age which people now call "street smart," that's who I was back then. Also, I may have missed a lot in academics, but I did not lack in the Performing Arts. I always participated in school programs. You would always see me dancing, singing, acting, and dressing as an angel for the live nativity scene during Christmas. I would hear my mother whine a little bit during those times because getting the white fabric for my angel costume meant she needed to put aside some extra change. Still, she talked about me very proudly to her co-sewers. I'm sure she sacrificed a meal or two just to get my costumes done.

I was a quiet and obedient student. I was not as aggressive and vocal as the others, but I knew I had enough confidence. I knew all my ABCs and numbers. I could write my name, and I remember reading some words. Maybe I got it easily, or the teacher was just teaching the same thing over and over. Well, who knows! My mother didn't check on us because she was busy working. All I know is I was always in school learning, selling goods, cleaning, grading papers, or doing whatever the teacher asked me to do. I remember my first grade teacher very clearly. She was huge! I never said it out loud, but oh boy! I need to describe her with words! God bless her! I'm not lying, she was quite heavy. She would always give me her yard stick so that I could lead the class with reading and counting while she sat and rested. I guess her weight bothered her. I knew some kids in my class who made funny faces and acted like they were measuring her butt size and legs with their imaginary measuring tape. I knew that what they were doing was bad, but I didn't do or say anything because I was just a passive little girl.

In our house, my least favorite thing was to do #2 because there was only one toilet, and it was outside the house. Like I said before, everyone in our household, including all the tenants, used this common bathroom/toilet. I remember being thankful for being constipated because I never liked using that toilet anyway. It would get all clogged up and nasty, especially during typhoon season. I guess the flood messed the pipelines or something. On some days, when I couldn't hold it any longer, *Papang* would spread some newspapers on the ground and instructed me to do it *there*.

Ha!

That was weird, but I did it anyway. Nature calls it. And when I'm done, I would wrap it up and find a safe place to discreetly dispose my waste. Oh well... it was better than seeing other people's junk in our toilet.

One day, while in class, my tummy started to growl. Then, it slipped!

Oops!

Too late!

One by one, my classmates started making comments about the funky smell.

My huge teacher asked, "*Sino umutot?*" ("Who farted?")

Nobody admitted it. Eventually, she figured it wasn't just a fart because the smell lingered. Aren't we lucky to have different scents of air freshener now? Imagine being the teacher in that room. You would be furious! I totally understand now what she felt at that time. Being a teacher for 30 years, I get it.

"*Sino ang tumae?*" ("Who pooped?"), she asked.

And still no reply.

With a loud voice, she asked the second time.

It startled me, so more of that stuff slipped off my butt.

"*Oh boy! This smells trouble.*" I mumbled.

Nobody admitted it, so it made the situation worse.

She said, "*Ayaw nyo umamin ha? Tingnan natin. Itong row na to, tayo!*" ("So nobody wants to admit it, huh? Now, let's see. This row, get up!")

She did it row by row, and everyone stood up but me.

Imagine the horror in my face in front of that fat and furious teacher while the rest of the class looked at me. My male seatmate looked at me with pity, but said nothing. He covered his nose, and I bet he would throw up if he breathed! My heart was pounding, and it almost fell off my chest. Everything faded in my sight. Now I know why my teacher didn't call *Mamang* or *Papang* to come pick me up, or at least send me to the nurse's office. Uhmm... we didn't have phones at that time, and we didn't have a nurse in school, I think. Or maybe my teacher didn't find anyone to send to notify my parents about my accident. Or, maybe I made her so mad that she just wanted to get rid of me. Next thing I know, I was walking home holding my skirt tightly around my legs to stop any "poop-pourrie" from falling.

Pause for a second.

Try to walk with your skirt hugging your legs.

It's not easy!

Try walking a little faster while looking down.

I walked the Hall of Shame.

I got home and went straight to the lone faucet outside our house. Around the faucet were some renters doing their laundry. *Mamang* saw me and asked what happened. I answered, "Well, I don't know. Some kid pooped on me by accident."

Oh well... I lied. I lied to save my dignity.

Mamang did not say anything, but I know she knew. Now that I have become a mother too, I know sometimes it is best not to say anything. Instead, *Mamang* helped me clean up.

I sat for a moment, and I wondered.
How can I go back to that room and lead the class?
It was humiliating.
It was very embarrassing.
It was degrading.
I was agonized with the feeling.

That was my very first sad experience as a kid.

2
CHAPTER

Childhood Taken Away

Christmas is my favorite holiday! Living in a Catholic country and having this special day as the longest celebrated holiday gives little kids the best time, and I mean *the best time!* Christmas begins on the very first day of September. We love the four **BER** months: Septem**ber**, Octo**ber**, Novem**ber**, and Decem**ber**! Lots of exchanging gifts and caroling. It is the time when kids make money. I'll explain. You form your own caroling group and decide who the lead singers are, the musicians, the treasurer/bucket holder, and the navigator. I was always in the front row because I was the dancer. Our plan was always to visit the "rich" first and then the "not-so- rich" last. We would go from house to house to sing carols, and they would give us coins. Each night, we emptied our buckets and split our income. Some audiences were generous, but of course, there will always be the not-so-generous ones who would close their doors. Some would even turn off their lights to avoid the pesky little annoying carolers! These not-so-generous people whose lights were turned off for most of the "–ber" months would turn on their lights ONLY on Christmas day, but still don't open their doors and act like nobody's home. As the song says, "Give love on Christmas day," some actually missed the message.

"Why are some people stingy?" This would be our hot topic while walking back home.

Well, it's ok. My *Papang and Mamang* would ask all three of us (*Ate, Kuya, and I*) to hang our socks (not the Christmas stockings that you see at the store, just our regular school socks) by the window on Christmas Eve. According to them, Santa would come by and put something in it if he thought we had been good kids.

We Asians don't have chimneys, but we do have open windows all day and all night as it is really hot in the Philippines. When I migrated to America, winter was almost unbearable for me. I was mighty COLD! My body has yet to adapt to the cold weather, even after being in the US for years. I still sleep in my pajamas, wrapped in my robe with knee-high socks, and a scarf! Yes, with a scarf at night! Don't accuse my husband of murder if I choke at night with that thing around my neck. I'm pretty sure he would be a potential suspect.

Just kidding!

I know he would never choke me to death. He loves me too much.

Anyway, back home, we would always get a few little toys and a couple of candies for Christmas. Nothing fancy like kids here in the USA get. Oh, the simple joys of poor little children in our country. Crayons, chocolates, apples... and guess what? I only got to eat an apple every Christmas!

Oh, how I used to nibble my apple because I wanted it to last longer. I knew it would take another year before I got to taste my favorite fruit again.

Surprisingly, when I came to Virginia in 2003, I tasted a REAL apple. I didn't know apples were so crunchy and juicy! The ones I had in the Philippines looked like apples but didn't taste like them at all! They were mushy. Oh well, at least I knew what apples *looked* like.

One time, I got a bar soap and a wash cloth for Christmas. It was a little insulting.

Do I smell bad?

Do I still stink from my accident when I was in the first grade?

We didn't have a nice bathroom with a shower, but I took a bath every day.

Wash cloth and soap for Christmas?

Who does that?

I wanted chocolates and candies!

Now that I have a family of my own, we started a tradition. On Thanksgiving Day, we decorate the house in the morning and cook dinner in the afternoon. My husband, who is into Christmas decorations, has it all planned out, and we just help him set things up. Every year, it reminds me that I never experienced all this as a child. We never had Christmas lights in our tiny house. My parents couldn't even afford to buy a single Christmas light. There was no extra money to pay for the electric bill. Plus, there was only one outlet, remember? But even if we did, Christmas lights were not a priority. We were busy thinking about where to get our food the next day. However, we never missed going to church for *Simbang Gabi,* the 9-day Novena before Christmas. We walked to church at dawn and attended the *Simbang Gabi* where we prayed for a Christmas miracle.

My mother, who was extremely busy at work, may have missed some Sunday masses, but she never ceased to pray. I would always see a rosary by her side, and she would hum church songs while doing work. I would go to the clothes factory where she worked, to help her cut up lengths of garter for the shorts. I would watch her tired body until she finally reached the last pair.

While we walked home, she would point to the barbeque stand with her lips. (If you Filipino readers can relate, say "Woot! Woot!" It's funny how we point with our lips. Go ahead and do it. I know you're doing it. It's a Filipino thing!)

She would say, *"Pag sweldo ko, bibili kita ng isang stick pero wag mo sabihin sa mga kapatid mo ha?"* ("When I get paid, I will buy you one stick of barbeque, but don't tell your older siblings, ok?")

For me, that was very special! It made me think I was her favorite because I was the baby.

We prayed the rosary as a family every night, and when we prayed, we couldn't sit or slouch. We knelt down with a straight body. We could sit on our knees for a minute to take a quick break, but we needed to go back up with folded hands. Sometimes, our prayer would get interrupted by farts, and we would just giggle. My mother also prays the entire Litany of Saints, with no shortcuts. My father, unlike my mom, was not very prayerful. He would listen then make comments trying to be funny.

He'd say, "*Ang dami namang peanut butter nyan! Peanut butter kayo ng peanut butter.*" ("That's a lot of peanut butter! You keep on saying peanut butter, peanut butter.")

(Peanut butter = pray for us)

I don't recall what the occasion was when the whole family went to an ice cream parlor. That was the happiest day of my childhood life with my parents and siblings. Unfortunately, that was the first and the last time. On our way home, I saw this pink dress, and I couldn't stop thinking about it. I really wanted that dress, so I cried and rolled on the sidewalk. I didn't stop. So *Mamang* bought two dresses: one for me and one for my sister, in the name of FAIRNESS. She bought us the dresses but warned us not to complain about not having food for a while.

We barely had anything to eat for weeks but hey, I was happy I got the dress. That was my first store-bought dress! MONUMENTAL, isn't it? I felt so pretty in it. What do you think?

Yup! My favorite pink dress, the reason why we ate Nissin ramen for days.

Then, things slowly changed. I would often hear my parents fighting in the middle of the night. Regularly, I would get awakened by screaming and crying. It wasn't clear to me why *Mamang* locked *Papang* in the room with one of our female tenants. I also wondered why he was even there in the first place. The next day, that lady moved out and another person came in. My father seemed to forget which door belonged to us. I bet he got confused as to which was ours.

Does he get lost in the middle of the night?

I wasn't sure.

Then my mom missed some days at work. She was groggy and pretty messed up.

Was she drunk?

I thought so.

I would see empty bottles of *Tanduay Rhum* in the morning. My mom did not sleep. She cried all night.

Why, you ask?

I don't know.

I was too young to put life's puzzle pieces together.

On some days, I would see flying plates and glasses heading towards my father. Oh goodness! He was good at ducking; he was never hit. I overheard my mom talking to one of the mothers in our area. The next day, I saw my father's nice-looking shirt cut into pieces!

It was like a confetti!

I wondered some more.

From what I heard, the shirt was my mom's birthday present to *Papang*. Apparently, someone from our small community saw my father having a date with one of our female tenants with that birthday shirt on.

That was wrong... So wrong!

I watched how things changed.

At one point, *Mamang* lost it and took a machete. She swung it around and aimed at *Papang's* shoulder. My father, God bless his soul, had surprising skills! He felt it coming and jerked to the left. The machete landed on the railing, bloodless!

Whoa!!

There was definitely divine intervention there!

Every day when I walked down the steps, I would feel the deep cut in that wounded wood. That machete could have cut his shoulder off, which could have meant some jail time for my mother. Well, no one went to jail, but no one wanted to say anything to anybody. Everyone seemed quiet.

That memory opened my eyes. I was young, but I knew what I wanted. That forced my young brain to think maturely. That was my defining moment. I made a pinky promise to myself: *When I grow up, I will marry someone who isn't like my father. I will marry someone who is religious, faithful and kind. I promise.*

With all the chaos and violence in our tiny home, I found myself walking to church on Sunday mornings. My siblings, I think, walked to church with their friends as well. Being the youngest child has pros and cons. You get special treatment from your parents but not so much from your older siblings. When my parents weren't looking, they would leave me alone. I guess they found me boring. I know they love me, but I was not a fun kid. I tattled A LOT! They did their thing with their friends, and I did my thing by myself. Sometimes, I would walk to church alone and sit there. I love the *Sermon* or the Homily as you call it. I was not a fan of the Readings because it had too many English words. My tiny brain could not fully understand what each Reading/Gospel meant. I could only appreciate it after the priest explained it in our language. There were times when I left the church with more questions than answers. The priest said, "Husbands, love your wives. Wives, love your husbands." But I didn't see that in my family. I witnessed cheating, fighting, lying, screaming, yelling, crying, and hurting. That's the kind of husband and wife I saw at home. I didn't know what was right. I was confused.

Then one night, *Mamang* said we were moving to the province—just us, without *Papang.*

What about my caroling group?

Who is going to be their dancer?

Who will be the angel next Christmas?

Who will sell the Nutribuns?

And grade the papers and water the plants?

What about my income and business?

And how about the boy who didn't laugh at me when I had that accident?

I think he had a crush on me, and I think I liked him too. He knew I was about to leave, so on Valentine's Day he came up to me and showed me something. It was a red tiny heart split into two. He put half of that heart on his chest, and put the other half on mine.

Isn't that sweet?

But then I had to leave, and I lost all that.

I felt like my childhood was snatched away from me.

3
CHAPTER

The Big Move

T he city bus stopped after about eight hours of quiet bus ride. We waited for the next ride to get to the town. I was tired and sleepy and did not pay attention to what was really happening. I think I just slept the whole trip. I woke up, and I heard different sounds. People were talking in different dialects. I opened my eyes, and I saw a different group of people. They were folks who you'd know at first glance are hardworking people. You don't need to know what they do for a living because their body shows it. They have thin but firm muscles. Their skin must have been exposed to the sun for years because they were burned and dried up like prunes. Their hands moved with the dexterity that comes with hard manual labor. Their feet were thick and ashy.

How did I know about their feet?

They didn't wear shoes.

Instead, they had *tsinelas* (flip flops).

They smelled like ocean and farm.

Finally, I woke up completely and realized I was now in a different world. We were waiting to be transferred to an island via a landing barge. There were two ways to get to the island: either get on the barge or rent a boat. We could have rented a boat, but *Mamang* thought it was wiser to save the money for something else, which made sense. I watched how the conductor's fat hands picked up rocks and laid them evenly to build a ramp between the barge and the shore. The driver and conductors worked together as a team to get their mini buses on that barge.

Decades later, when my husband and I went to Williamsburg, VA with our Child #5, I was amazed at how this whole process was so quick and easy.

Where were our other children, you ask?

Oh, they were busy with school, work, sports, and friends.

Only the youngest child is living with us now, but we make the most of what we have. Being the cheap family that we are, we are always on the hunt for something to do that is free but still fun. One of these activities was driving to Williamsburg and getting on a barge. I watched how cars got on and off in an instant. Everything was just automatic!

Imagine what this woman from a third world country felt like in a first world country! Everything looked so magical! Praise the Lord, Alleluia! That moment brought back memories from four decades ago. But guess what? Life got better in my little hometown. They no longer have to make a ramp from rocks because now, they a have a bridge that connects the mainland to our island. God bless the people who initiated that project and the people who put that bridge together. It's like a bridge to Heaven!

Anda Bridge

Back to my story, the next day, *Mamang* walked me to my new school. I was introduced to my new class, and I smiled a little. It felt weird. My new classmates looked and smiled back at me. Surprisingly, I was one of the few students with shoes on! Now that was awkward. I felt like a city girl for the first time. To add to that fancy feeling, *Mamang* brought two bottles of *Coke litro* and some ham sandwiches because it was my birthday! The class sang me the usual birthday song, and I was welcomed warmly in my new environment. That day, over 40 years ago, was the first time I had a birthday party. I hadn't had one before it, but I was okay. My life went on as normal. I never realized what I was missing as a child because I never had much anyway. I didn't realize that I just moved to a more difficult situation. I wasn't aware I was that poor because I was happy no matter what.

The following day, I decided to go to school in flip flops so that I could blend in. I met more friends, and got to know more teachers, and I played with my newfound friends in the field. We didn't have a gym class because we didn't have a gym.

Haha!

But what we did have was this assembly area in front of the stage where the school principal would launch a contest for all the students. It was called, "The Weed Game."

Wait.

It's not what you think—let me explain.

Every year, we held intramurals of different sports. Schools from various *barrios* or counties competed against each other. Mine was the most elite school in our town, mind you. It was and still is the center of all the elementary schools in our municipality. Anyway, to prepare for big sports events, we needed to help clean up the premises. There was no such thing as lawn mowers in our school district during my time. Instead, there were multiple human-powered lawn hands to straighten up the field. From the stage, the principal said something to this effect: ***"The one with the most weed wins!* Ready, set, go!"**

So all of us elementary students bolted to the field, gathered as much grass and weeds as our tiny hands could possibly hold, and ran back in front of the stage. With all the sweat and sunburn, we presented our weeds. I had no idea if there was a proclaimed winner, or if it was just a trick. Who knows! I didn't care. I knew I had the best time. Then I played volleyball and tried track and field. Track wasn't fun for me. Gradually, the sad memories from that big city school changed to loving the fun life with my newfound county friends.

I went to Anda Central School, but we lived in San Nicholas. It was the closest *barrio* to the City Hall, a little over a mile from home. Since it is within walking distance, I walked to school with my friends in the morning and marched back home after class. At lunch time, my buddies from where I lived stayed in the building because they had packed lunch. Meanwhile, I would go home because there was nothing to pack in the first place. My mother, who at that time was adjusting to our new life and finding ways to feed her three children, used to walk around and look for something to cook while I was at school. Incredibly, she would have the food ready before I came home at noon. When days were rough, I would come home and just eat rice and the worst kind of *bagoong* (fermented anchovies)—the cheapest meal ever. That was what she could only afford. I would see her buy the kind with wiggly worms, but pick them out, strain it, save its *juice,* and sauté it with garlic and vinegar to kill the germs. She said it has been taken care of. She says they're the good kind of worms anyway. She must have been right because I have a great immune system! I've never had any serious health issues, only the regular colds, headaches, and fevers, which happen rarely. Thank God for those little jiggles!

Sometimes life would beat us so hard that we barely had anything to eat. We were lucky to have just rice on the table—I mean on a plastic plate. I remember, we actually did NOT have a table. We just had to sit on the floor and eat with our bare hands. While I don't remember crying and feeling sorry for myself, I remember crying because my lips were sore and chapped.

I think consuming that *bagoong* every day, three times a day tore up my fat chunky lips! They hurt so bad that you would want to skip chewing.

It stings!

I didn't want to talk much because when I did, my lips touched.

That was torture!

If I needed to talk, I did it without moving my lips.

Now, I challenge you readers to talk with your lips open.

Say, "Thank you God for the rice on my plate."

It's not easy, right?

After my meal, I would rush back to school for my afternoon classes. That mid-day walk dehydrated me. Thank God I had my one-of-a-kind water bottle. While my classmates had the real ones with cute cartoon pictures around it, mine was unique because it was a recycled ketchup bottle.

Resourceful, eh!

During the weekends, *Mamang* and I would get up early to fix our lunch basket and walk a couple of miles to meet up with the other folks and happily "hang out" in the middle of the field while planting rice and exchanging jokes to lighten up the long day of bending over. My children learned the song *Planting Rice* for the annual Filipino Festival here in Richmond, VA. Part of the song goes, "Planting rice is never fun..." and I tell them, "It was not fun at all." We didn't wear gloves or boots, so at the end of the day, we rinsed our mud-coated fingers and toes while feeling the backache that ran from our neck down to the butt area. After the harvest season, we would get up early (again) to secure a spot near the municipal hall plaza to dry the *palay* (unhusked rice). The mid-day sun hit that area perfectly and was the best place for this task. In the morning, we spread out our DIY *tarp* or quilted flour bags, and carefully poured bag after bag of rice then returned to scoop them back in the bags before the sunset. We went through this process maybe twice before we bring them to the milling station. If there was not enough money, we pounded the rice using a paddle-like material. Then we put it in a *bilao*, a large woven winnowing basket, and tossed it up and down. This separated the chaff from the rice. This works best on a windy day because the chaff just flies out as you toss the rice in the air.

If we were not working in the field, *Mamang* would drag me to different barrios with the statue of Mary wrapped in her arms even on a rainy day. Every October, the month of the Holy Rosary, we would walk from one barrio to another to deliver the statue of Mama Mary to the family who had agreed to keep her for the week. We would consider ourselves lucky if we just prayed the rosary with the family because otherwise, we would stay a little longer and tutor them.

So tell me. Where can I find time to hang out with friends?

Then my skin changed. My skin got so dark and so dry. I realized I now looked like one of the prune-looking guys I saw that first time I got off the bus. Do you want to know what was worse than that? They had shiny bronzed smooth skin, but I had a pimply round oily face. Even though my arms and legs were so dry, my face was always greasy. My cheeks were entirely covered with pimples and acne. I tried to squeeze them, but they bled, and they sometimes had pus!

I looked really gross.

Disgusting.

I didn't even want to look at myself in the mirror. I was an oily, jack-fruit-looking, red-faced little girl. Also, my family didn't use shampoo. Or toothpaste. I lost my confidence, but I was happy when I was with my friends. No one judged me. They still liked me. I was glad I met some accepting class-mates in my new planet.

I also joined the Girl Scouts Club. My favorite was camping trips! When I say camping, I mean *real* camping. We didn't have the store-bought tents. We made our own tents. We would gather tree branches to hold our DIY tents made out of rice and flour bags. Then, we would go around to collect some hay or grass to cover the rocky surface. This served as a cushion before we spread out our blankets. Next, we built a fire to cook our food using tins as pots. There was no electricity, but it was fun!

Now, my family goes on camping trips every summer. Sometimes, when the weather is nice, we would put up our tents in our backyard on weekends. And every summer, my husband would whine about it asking, "Why do we have to sleep in tents when we have beds in the house?" Then my children would reply: "Because Mama misses being poor!"

Don't get me wrong here. I am far from being rich, but at least everything seems stable. There's food when you're hungry. There's a bathroom available for everyone. I don't need to walk to school because I have a car to drive. Life became pretty convenient here in America. So sometimes I do really miss that kind of special feeling—the feeling of discomfort because it reminds me of life—a life that is challenging, but in every challenge, that's where God is. To me, that is a wondrous thing.

Then, my mom got into the trading business. She planted rice for other people's fields, and when the harvest time came, she would get her share. I know we had enough rice for the year, but we never had much *ulam* (viand)— this is something or anything that you eat with rice. It could be vegetables, meat, or fish. My daily *ulam* was that worst *bagoong. Mamang* would sell a portion of her harvest to buy us some meat or exchange it with fish to give us a break from *bagoong.* Life got a little better. She got us a small house. Nothing fancy. No realtor. No closing costs. No title. No insurance. No mortgage. It was just 800 pesos (about $20)—fully paid. That was our first real property! My mother did all that without my father. She's a very strong-willed woman. So we lived in that bamboo house sitting on four stilts. It had a five-step ladder, but at the end of the ladder was a wall.

Where's the door, you ask.

It's on the other wall!

How do you get to the door, then?

You must hug the wall at the top of the ladder and slowly move your legs as you hold on to each corner of the partition. Focus your eyes at the other side, then slowly jump a little to get to the floor. Finally, waiting for you is the door without a knob.

Alright!

This sounds complicated.

I'll help you imagine this.

Have you seen Spiderman?

That's how we looked when we got in and out of our house—like a bunch of Spidergirls.

Did we ever invite friends and other relatives to come over?

NO! They were not skillful enough!

But there was an outdoor receiving area for our clumsy guests. They waited down the steps or sat on a bamboo bench under the tree.

Was there power and water in that house?

NO!

My siblings and I each made our own gas lamp. You can customize it to suit your lifestyle. If you want to do homework at night, you should make the wick bigger to give you more light. Otherwise, keep it small. *Mamang* loved that because it consumed less gas.

One time, I found a book. It was a fiction book. It had no front cover and some pages were missing. Also, the pages might have been white at one point, but when I found it, the pages were already yellow and crisp. I borrowed it and read it at night by the light of my personal lamp. I was so into it, especially when Pinocchio's nose got longer each time he lied.

Do you know that feeling when you're watching a movie on Netflix and the screen freezes or the Wi-Fi acts up just when you were getting to the most exciting part?

Ugh!

That's what it felt like to read my book!

I got to the part when Pinocchio's nose was growing, and then the next three pages were missing.

What?

Where is page 102?

Why did it jump to page 105?

What happened to Pinocchio?

Then, I heard a buzz and smelled something weird. My face was too close to the flame, and I had burnt my bangs while I was reading! That's terrible, isn't it?

How will I go to school the next day with burnt bangs?

And where will I find the missing pages?

Oh well, I just made predictions. I went ahead and read page 105. As I continued, I found more missing pages in the next few chapters. Well, at least I enjoyed reading. That was actually the first book that I have ever read.

Anyway, have I mentioned that we didn't have a source of water in our house?

We got water in the well from my auntie's house across the street.

How did we bring the water up the house when you had to hug the wall to get in the house?

You need teamwork!

While one sibling stays on the ground and holds the bucket up, another sibling is up inside the house to grab it. Since I was the youngest and littlest, I couldn't do all that. I did, however, help with other chores like washing dishes and making the lamp. We didn't have any toys, but we still had fun. I wonder why we didn't have TV when we were in the stilt house—uhmmm—we didn't have electricity! Yeah, that's why I made lamps, duh! But one thing we did have was a *transistor radio*. That was our major source of entertainment. That's where we listened to the afternoon drama series, *SIMATAR!* It used six D batteries which should last for a couple of weeks. If you start hearing the characters talk like aliens, then that means your batteries are low. What we would do was take the batteries out and let them sit under the sun for a day. Then we would put them back in before our show, and voilà! Fully-charged batteries! We would throw them away only when they started to water.

I figure you have a burning question: What about the bathroom?

Of course, we had one! Are you kidding me?

There was an extension on the other side of the house where the door was located. It was an open space, with no roof. This was where we washed the dishes, cooked rice and do number 1. When it rained, it rinsed the dishes, but we couldn't cook because the firewood would get wet. On the other hand, rain was great because it cleared out the urine smell. So, it's good and bad.

What about if we do number 2?

What's the strategy for that?

Girl, it's easy!

Go to the woods, and do your business. We kind of marked our territory there, so it's all good.

Did we complain?

NO!

Were we grateful?

Yes! Very grateful, and we thanked God every day!

Sometimes during the weekends, I would walk a mile to check if the house near the City Hall had their windows open. If they were watching my favorite afternoon variety show, *Eat Bulaga,* I would come by their yard and watch it from the outside. I loved the dance contest, and the hosts were just too funny! Then one time, someone went in my direction and closed the window that I was looking through. Oh no! They didn't want me standing there. I turned around speechless. How would I know who won the weekly finals?

I took a deep sigh and mumbled, "Oh well...I hope my favorite dance group gets it."

I walked back home with a heavy heart.

I whispered to myself, "One day... one day... I will buy my own TV and will never have to walk and watch from other people's house."

Then, it was time for my auntie and her three children to migrate to Hawaii. My uncle, who was in the military, petitioned them. Her two older children, however, needed to stay and wait for a little longer because they were over 18 years old. My auntie asked *Mamang* to take charge of their properties. So she sold the stilt house, and we moved into their concrete house. It felt so good—it was a real house with two bedrooms, a basement, a kitchen, a living room, a detached bathroom, a pigpen, and a covered well with a pump.

Wow! That was total upgrade!

My auntie's family owned several rice fields. *Mamang* was tasked to take care of my auntie's two older children who were in college at that time. However, my mom and my two older cousins didn't get along well, so we had to step down and move to the pigpen while they stayed in the house.

YES!

We lived in the pigpen.

I was in high school then. Every summer, I would go back to the city and work in my other maternal auntie's factory. She married an engineer. Apparently, my mom has some well-off siblings. According to her, there were 12 of them in total. It's funny how she explained the pattern of how they were all born... ugly-pretty-ugly-pretty. Unfortunately, *Mamang* fell on the ugly side while her sisters, who were on the pretty side, were blessed enough to marry handsome and educated men. The pretty faces became wealthy even without a college education. My mom, who was on the ugly side but had the prettiest heart, God bless her hardworking heart, married a security guard. Neither of them finished high school.

Also, while kids my age enjoyed their summer playing, I was out in the city working in my auntie's factory. On weekdays, I sewed bonnets, baby shoes, or onesies, and got paid by the dozen. On weekends, my auntie would pick me up at 3 a.m., so we could set up her baby products in the market. We stayed there and sold until about 2 p.m. Then we would pack up and try to be home around 4 p.m. While most teenagers sleep in on weekends, I was out working from dawn to late afternoon but hey, that's worth 25 pesos (50 cents). Well, as the old people would always say, teenagers eat a lot because they are in their growing years. I would have loved to devour everything, but I didn't have anything to eat. Thankfully, my auntie gave me some change, so I could get some *lugaw* (rice porridge) at the market cafeteria for lunch. I was fine with doing this if it wasn't raining, but when it rained, there was just too much work. We made a roof to keep the merchandise from getting wet, but sometimes, they still got soaked when the downpour came with strong winds.

Oftentimes, I couldn't help but question myself, "Why am I doing this? Why can't I stay in bed and sleep for as long as I want? Do I really need to wake up this early to earn a living? I'm tired, sleepy, and hungry! Shouldn't parents be providing for their children?"

Maybe yes, to some privileged kids, I suppose, but not to me. I needed to do this to earn money. I didn't have time to relax and enjoy my teenage years because I was always working. I know it's bad to be jealous, but I get really jealous sometimes when I see my children living a life that I wished I had. They are enjoying their lives. When they come up to me and ask if they can hang out with their friends, it makes me wonder what *hanging out* really means. It must be fun to *hang out* with friends and enjoy good food. My definition of *hanging out*? *Hanging out* some baby products in the market to sell or setting up a cover to make a roof when it rained.

Sometimes, I would go see my other beautiful auntie who married an architect. I would spend the whole summer there and help take care of my cousin. She is the only female daughter and the youngest in their family. I looked forward to spending time with her because I got to eat food that I had never tasted in my life! They used to have pizza, grapes, milk, chocolates, cheese curls... all that good stuff! They would order pizza but unfortunately, no extra slice would be left for me. But it was alright. I watched them eat and waited. When they finished, I would help the maids clean up and discreetly throw in my mouth the pizza crusts that were left in the box.

I loved it when we went grocery shopping! It was heaven! I also enjoyed watching my cousin dance her ballet and complete her swimming lessons.

Sometimes I wonder what lessons I would have taken if I had the chance. I think I would have liked to wear those tutus.

There were times when I asked God why they had all this, and we didn't. Then, I would reset my brain and just focus on thanking God because at least I knew what it looked like.

Now I know why I loved summer so much! When school started in June, my classmates in the province noticed a special glow on my face. According to them, every summer, my cheeks were rosy, and my skin was a little moist. Well, it's because I was well-fed and had consumed some healthy food. They had milk that made my skin glow a little bit. In contrast, my family's *bagoong* with worms had dried my face. And there was no milk in our pigpen house. Still no electricity. What dried my skin even more was the water from the well. Sometimes, a frog would fall in and drown. When you get water and smell the dead frog, it means you need to boil your water before drinking it. This is why I never liked frogs! Swollen lips and dead frogs in your water was NOT heavenly at all.

There were some boys in my class who used to follow me around as I walked home with my walking buddies. I didn't know if they knew I lived in a pigpen. I can't be sure, but I'm guessing they thought I lived in my auntie's concrete house. No one would think we lived there unless you went in the property and saw it for yourself. Honestly, I liked talking to those boys too, but what if they find out I lived in the pigpen? That's a major turn off, right? If I invite them over, where would they sit? Probably on a rock because we didn't have a couch, not even a chair. We sit on our wooden beds. In high school, I felt like I needed a father, a male figure. At that time, I was very insecure because I felt like these guys wouldn't take me seriously if there was no male figure in my life. I thought I needed a security guard. I knew my father was not faithful, and maybe not as responsible as the other fathers out there, but I never saw him put his hands on my mother. He would only duck to avoid the flying dishes. And he never yelled or screamed back at my mom. He would just turn around and walk away. I bet he knew he was in the wrong after all. My mom was the screamer and the violent one. Well, she had her reasons why she did what she did. That was their problem, and when I was a teenager, I also had my own problems.

The next summer, when I went to work at my auntie's factory again, I saw *Papang*. He was living alone. I thought he might have gotten tired of womanizing, so I talked to him and invited him to come and join the rest of us in the pigpen. He left his job and came home with me, against my mother's wishes. She was not pleased with what I did, but *Papang* tried to win her back. He did whatever she asked of him. He went out planting rice with my mom. He went fishing with my uncles. He fetched water from the well for us. Every morning, he would get me a bucket of water for my daily bath before I went to school. God knows he tried, but I think there was just so much hate in *Mamang's* heart. There were days when I woke up hearing their heated arguments about the past. I started to blame myself. It was my fault. I was selfish to think about myself and invited him over. I was selfish because I did not consider *Mamang's* feelings. I got tired of the fighting, so I ran away. During that time, I felt like I hated my parents! I wished I had a different mother and father.

When I left, I went to the convent. After a week, they came to pick me up, but I refused. I needed a break. I loved my new place. It was quiet, calm, peaceful, and I became more prayerful. And yes, they did have electricity there. I wanted to become a nun. I wanted to be alone with God and forget about my messed up life. Then, Sister Norie, one of the nuns there, talked to me. I forgot what her exact words were, but ultimately, I decided to come home, and I felt so much better.

Life went on. I was 14 years old, and I had really good friends. In high school, there were three different groups of students: there were those who lived in *babale* (upper-class students with educated parents and lived in normal houses), those who lived further down in the *barrios*, and finally, there was my group: those who lived not too far and not too near—just right, maybe about a mile from all the main stores and Town Hall. Our school had no library, but it was next to our church. I studied in a Catholic school. On Saturday afternoons, we would help clean the church and make sure everything was in place for the Sunday morning service. I joined the choir, too. There was not a lot of resources in our one and only building. This building held 1st to 4th year high school students. My friends and classmates from where I lived would share books. Those who lived in the same area used one set of books, and those who lived on the other side of town shared a different set of books.

YOU ARE NOT ALLOWED TO WRITE ON THE BOOKS!

You would have to pay a penalty. Books are for reading only. My two best friends (Mario Capa and Teresa Atizora) and I used to sit in the shed and do homework together. For study breaks, we would go around and pick up whatever fruits were available that season to snack on.

Sodas, chips, cookies, muffins, and cakes were all foreign to me. Instead, we would get *kaimitos, aratiles,* star fruit, or mangoes to chew on. It was a lot of fun to climb and pick fruits in each other's backyards. We would use our skirts to catch the fruits. And oh boy, I made sure I had on decent underwear when I did that. I didn't want to be judged for wearing *hole-y* panties. I always wished I would receive a new set of hand-me-down clothes and shoes from somewhere. I wanted to be a little stylish too when I went to church.

One time, our parish priest planned a concert to raise funds because we wanted a marble-floored church. So, we practiced and practiced. That was a big event, so I pleaded with *Mamang* to buy me some real clothes—*clothes* that actually fit me. I wanted at least two, so I didn't look the same to the people who decided to watch the concert on both days. Thank God! After 10 years, I got my second store-bought clothes! I thank Fr. R. for initiating that concert. If not for him, I wouldn't have known what it felt like to have brand new clothes at age 14.

Back then, I didn't realize our bodies would change around my age. When my children used to give me a paper to sign to give them permission to attend Family Life at their school, I was confused. In the school where I came from, I figured out my own life. There was no Family Life Class or Career Day—nothing (but I did learn to gut a fish at school). One day, I was out of town with my volleyball team for competition. (By the way, during our time, if you played sports, be prepared to play in the sun. We had no indoor gym, so we played out in the open field! No roof, no water fountain, just a concrete court and a net.) I had been in the sun for the whole day and when I went to the bathroom, I saw blood! I panicked and got scared. I didn't tell anybody, but I was thinking, "*When did I hurt myself? How did I cut myself? Did I stay too long in the sun? I didn't know volleyballs could cut you!*"

How ignorant of me!

Yes, I was blindsided because nobody told me I could be a lady anytime soon! Nobody mentioned that girls would get their period at some point in their lives. I believe my mother forgot to tell me about this because she was busy making a living while also fighting with my father. Anyway, I would make my own washable pads every month. I only started using the real pads when I was in college. Yup! I made DIY pads. If you want to learn more, email me at austaana@yahoo.com. That was one big bump to deal with growing up. I wish I knew. I wish someone had told me. I wished someone had shown me how to take care of myself. Nobody did, but it's ok. I figured it out by myself anyway.

It was Junior Senior Prom. Everybody was talking about their dresses, which all looked pretty. Meanwhile, my dress was something made by *Mamang*. I wished I had another store-bought or made-to-order gold dress but nope... she had already spent a lot of money for my choir dresses. She made me a pretty ok dress, but I still wished it was a store-bought one. The boy who had a big crush on me was my partner. I have no idea how we used to get our partners. Was it assigned? I don't know. My children would sometimes talk about how a certain girl was asked to attend the prom or how this girl asked this boy to go to the dance/prom. We didn't have all that. You were lucky to be at the prom, period!

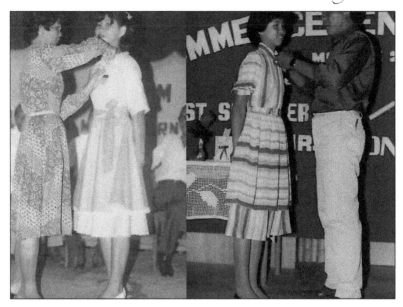

Meet my *Papang* and *Mamang*. This is my awards day dress and yellow prom dress, both made by *Mamang*.

But we did have some sleepovers. Yay! I loved sleepovers because I got to see my friends' houses. They had real houses, unlike ours. Also, they had real families, with parents who got along and decent food in their kitchen. They had refrigerators and TVs. They had electricity and real bathrooms inside their house. My friends didn't have to go to the woods when they had to do number 2. I bet they didn't use DIY sanitary pads either. Wow! They had all that, and we didn't. That was the kind of family that I would like to be a part of—not like mine. Thank you Vangie Carolino and Tina Celino for sharing your homes with me.

I didn't have a toothbrush.

How about toothpaste, did you have toothpaste?

Not until the end of my junior year, I think?

Lesson 101: How to brush your teeth without a toothbrush and toothpaste?

Oh, go find a guava tree. Break a twig and take the bark off at the tip. Then, push it against the table and soften the strands in the twig to make bristles. Now, you have a DIY toothbrush!

How does it work?

Oh, you wet the bristles and dip it on a plate with rock salt. Gum bleeding is common when you do this. The cruel rock salt cuts your baby gums.

Did we complain?

No.

Were we thankful?

Yes!

Thank you, God, for giving us creative minds.

If you think your cavities are building up, gargle with salt and vinegar. It does work! Also, I used to wonder why my classmates from *babale* (center of the town) had nice smooth hair. I found out they used shampoos—of course, I didn't. I used the laundry bar soap to wash my face and hair. My hair was stiff and sticky. I couldn't even run a comb in my hair because it was clumped up. Then I was told that the bar soap made my pimples get worse because it was too strong for my face. They suggested "Perla" soap, which was still a laundry soap but milder, but still nothing really happened. I got tired of my pimples because they wouldn't leave me alone! But I wore clean crisp uniforms. Every weekend, I would fill up our heavy metal iron with charcoal. I tried not to press my uniform on a windy day because the wind caused the debris to get in my white blouse. Yes, I was a poor girl and may have been hungry most of the time, but I always wore a clean, pressed uniform to school. It gave me confidence.

Then, I was a senior. Graduating students needed to take the NCEE (National College Entrance Examination). It was a big test to determine if you could pursue a 4-year degree or a 2-year vocational course. I wanted a 4-year degree, no matter what it was! I wanted to go to college. I wanted to go to the big city and compete with the city girls. Year after year, my mom would go up the stage to get my awards at the awards assemblies. I was one of the academically strong students in our little town. Before taking the NCEE test, *Papang* took one of his chickens, fried it and cooked it for me.

I asked why.

Mamang answered, "You need some brain food. The *bagoong* won't be of any help to your brain, so we figured we need to feed you some good food for your test."

I thought that was *manna from heaven above.* I wished I took this test every day, so I could enjoy a sumptuous meal. And I did pass the test! Thank you for the chicken thigh and leg, I could take a 4-year course! Then one night, *Mamang* told me I couldn't go to college because they didn't have enough money to send me to school. She told me that I would have to wait for my older sister to finish before I went. My brother went to live with my auntie, the one who married an architect. Her husband was his godfather. He went to college to pursue engineering but dropped out because his girl-friend got pregnant, and they needed to get married. I couldn't believe what I was hearing. I cried through my sleepless nights. There was a typhoon, a Signal #3. I sobbed while I watched the lightning hit the night. I sobbed as I heard the thunder boom over our pigpen house. I couldn't sleep because I was thinking about how doomed I was. I couldn't sleep because the rain got inside our three-walled house.

Yes! Three walls.

Shouldn't houses have four walls?

That's what I thought, but ours only had three.

What about the bugs and mosquitoes?

Well, we had mosquito nets. At night, I hung it over my wooden bed. But it didn't give 100% protection because they snuck in my bed crevices. Sometimes, I would sleep soundly and lean on the net unconsciously. Oh! The mosquitoes loved that! They devoured my arms and legs.

Picture this: a girl with a greasy pimply face, stiff clumped hair, yellow jagged teeth with bleeding gums, covered with sore fat chunky lips, and dark dried up skin with bug bites.

What a great life for a 16-year-old girl, right?

Eventually, I got tired of crying and wanted to sleep, but I couldn't. My bamboo bed and sheet were wet and cold. I was wet and cold too. I couldn't even lean on the wall because water seeped in as it had tiny holes. It was a wall made of woven coconut leaves. I pushed my bed to the center of the room. There, I sat thinking about the whole situation. I didn't want to live this life forever. I knew I could do something. But if I didn't go to college, I'd be stuck in this town and end up selling fish in the market. Or I might marry a fisherman or a farmer, and there goes the same story. I didn't want to end up like my parents. I was crushed and broken but determined to do something for myself. My mother's voice telling me that I couldn't go to college echoed like thorns around my head.

I felt like my dreams were shattered and the lightning has hit my future.

4
CHAPTER

The Big Comeback to the City

At 16 years old, I graduated high school as the second best in class—
Salutatorian as they called it. No big deal, there's only a little over 20
students in my senior class. Besides, so what? My parents were not sending
me to college anyway. What's going to happen to me? I closed my eyes and
pictured myself, either selling fish in the market on Fridays or planting rice
in the fields all day long.

By the way, the market opens only once a week, on Fridays. That day is
the most fun day in our town. It's when people from different counties go
to the "city" and do their grocery shopping. Vendors from different neigh-
boring towns outside the island also come by to give us, *Andanians,* more
choices. It's like imported goods. That's where I got my two store-bought
dresses for the two-day concert. Mind you, I wore imported dresses, and
I felt confident. Over the years, I learned that confidence is like an outfit.
It is something that you need to put on. It's not always in your system.
Confidence wears off, and when it does, you have an option to put it back
on or not.

Upon graduating from high school, I felt no confidence at all. Most of
my close friends were set to pursue their college degree in better and more
civilized towns the following school year. As a tradition, college students
come home during major holidays: Semestral break in November (All Saints'

Day and All Souls' Day), Christmas in December, and Holy Week in April. During those breaks, all *bakasyonistas and kolehialas* (tourists and college kids) see each other in two places: the church and the market. This is when parents proudly brag about how their kids are doing at their respective colleges (give this moment to the parents, for their children are their most valued possessions). And the college kids look very different after a year or two. They look more sophisticated. They wore more trendy clothes. They speak Tag-lish (mix of Tagalog and English), making them sound "classier." Townspeople look at them from head to toe and toe to head not to size them up, but to awe and admire. The locals took pride in the returnees' accomplishments.

How about me?

I was stuck. I didn't want to be on the looking-at-people-with-awe-and-admiration side. I wanted to be on the people-being-looked-at-with-awe-and admiration side.

I thought to myself, *I know I can do something. I know I can be a better person. I know I can be somebody. I know I can help my parents. I don't want to be this poor forever. I want to eat something other than rice and salt, or rice and bagoong. I want to dress up. I want some brand-new shoes, not just hand-me-downs.*

My husband and children always wondered why my toes look like ginger. I explained, "I never had shoes that really fit me, ok?" I always waited for donations. If there was something that came my way but was a little small, I figured out a way to slide my feet in and made it work. I crunched my toes at the end and walked slowly to minimize friction with the tight shoes. Imagine the comfort that I get at the end of the day when I kicked my shoes off. But I don't really *kick* those tight shoes off—I am thankful for them even if they made my feet sore and calloused. If you get a chance, take a look at my feet. No amount of pedicures could fix them.

One summer, some of my aunties came to town to celebrate Holy Week. Days before their scheduled drive back to Manila, I asked if I could get a ride to the mainland. Luckily, there was one spot available all the way in the back of their van. I stayed in one of my auntie's place for a few days. This is not the engineer or architect's wife. From what I know, she was the wife of a businessman. They had two children at that time, one boy and one girl.

With courage and confidence, I talked to my businessman uncle, "Do you need a *yaya* (a stay-in babysitter) for my cousin? I think I'll make a good *yaya*. You don't need to pay me, though. I just need a place to stay because I want to go to college. If you want, you pay my tuition, and I will take care of your children and do ALL the chores."

He agreed. He gave me 2,000 pesos (about $45) cold cash for the first semester. I got a good deal.

The next day, I went to the nearest college, Pasig Catholic College. It caters to students from kindergarten to college and is adjacent to the church. I entered the gate, and I saw different lines for registration. There were two lines that caught my eye—one with a sign that said "BSE" and another, "BEEd."

I mumbled, "Hmmmm, I wonder what that's all about."

Then, I figured, who cares? You want to go to college? Here you are in a college campus.

I picked the longer line. I thought that since it was longer, it must be better. I paid and left. I went home and did my chores. I also got two sets of uniforms. Yes, we wore uniforms in that Catholic school, matched with a pair of flat shoes, and guess what? Those shoes really fit me! They were store-bought shoes and not hand-me-downs. And my uniforms, they were fit to my size. Talk about an instant life upgrade! This is it! My life has changed.

Thank you, Uncle!

I am now a college girl. Unbelievable!

I knew it. I knew I can do something other than sell fish. My gut told me I could do something with my life.

First day in college, and what a bummer! I read the syllabus and course outline.

This is education class? I am enrolled in Elementary Education? I will be a teacher here? **NOOOOOOOOO!**

Pictures of my fat teacher from first grade danced in my head. This can't be real. I never dreamed of becoming a teacher. I didn't want to sell *yema* (milk candies) or *pastillas* (milk sticks). I didn't want to grade test papers. I wanted to dress up and wear different shoes. I wanted to be in the corporate world, bumping into cute guys in their suit and tie or become a flight attendant walking tall and pretty while pulling my luggage, and hopefully, marry a handsome pilot, or find my childhood crush in the province, the son of the mayor.

Please, God! I don't want to be a teacher!

I think God whispered, "Alright, girl, a teacher or a farmer? Now you choose."

Ok, alright, Lord. I made some modifications to my plan: be a teacher for five years, save up, and then go to some airline school.

Freshman year had its ups and downs. The ups were: I saw different lifestyles and study habits, went to church every day, met new friends, enjoyed an actual library, loved my professors, and admired the senior Education students. I wanted to be like them one day. The downs: I didn't have time to sit and do homework after school. I was always busy cooking, cleaning, washing dishes, ironing, and doing laundry manually. My uncle who provided for my tuition didn't have a washing machine. You should have seen my bleeding hands. There was just too much laundry to wash for my 16-year-old body. There was not a day that I didn't feel tired. I didn't eat *bagoong* every day, but I was always hungry because there wasn't much food left for me when I got home at midnight.

A typical day for me looked like this: I drop off my cousin at school at 7:30 am, do all my chores until 11:30 am, pick up my cousin, feed her, then I take a bath at 12:10 pm. By 12:30, I should be on my daily jeepney commute for my 1:00 pm class. My last class ends around 11:00 pm and then I commute back home. Traffic gets really bad at night. I should be home before midnight, and I was often greeted by a bunch of dirty dishes in the sink. Dishwashers were not a thing in the Philippines—well, at least in my world. Still in uniform, I find myself washing the dishes and hoping that there's a little bit of rice left for me. There's nothing. I had no choice but to sleep with an empty stomach. I drink water, though. It helped. It's a lot better than drinking water from the well with dead frogs (I still hate those frogs!) Well, I should be done with the dishes at 1:00 a.m. But sometimes my businessman uncle (may he rest in peace), would come home with something to cook. He would ask me to stay up a little longer to clean the fish and cook it, because he was hungry after work. I looked forward to having a meal before my bedtime, but when everything is cooked, my young and worn-out body couldn't stay up any longer. I wake up the next day still feeling hungry. Sometimes, I didn't feel like a family member. I always saw myself as their slave, but not really because they sent me to school, and I had a place to stay.

I didn't have a bedroom. Instead, I had a ripped folding bed. It was so ripped that my back was an inch away from the floor. At least it was better than my bamboo bed back home. I waited for everyone to settle down before I set my bed because I slept in the hallway, and I didn't want to be in people's way. On a rainy day, I couldn't sleep on it because water dripped exactly where my bed was. One time, I woke up wet and soggy in the middle of the night. I was too tired to change my clothes, so I just put a bucket out to catch the dripping water. Then, I folded my bed, put it on its side, sat next to it, leaned on it, and slept. Thank God I didn't catch any colds or a cough. God made me a tough chick!

On nights when there was too much going on in that house, I would tiptoe and go to the vacant house which was my other auntie's house. The aunt who married an architect owned it, but they had moved to a much bigger place. They kept the house key placed in a common area for anyone who might need a place to stay. That became my place. I sometimes used one of its rooms at night. It felt so good to have a quiet place. At my bedside was my little *Sto. Niño* and a rosary; these were my night buddies. I never failed to pray before sleeping. And every night, I wore my little light orange jacket under my blanket. I couldn't sleep without a blanket. It gives me security. It gives me privacy because when I slept on the aisle, people just walked by me. I covered my whole body with my blanket, so I couldn't see anybody, even though it could be suffocating during summertime. Did I mention there was no fan or air conditioner? Yes! It was hot, but I wrapped myself like a burrito. The blanket was my hiding place.

Anyway, one time in that vacant house, I woke up in the middle of the night, and it was very dark. I tried to turn my body to the other side, but I couldn't. I tried to get up, but I couldn't. I opened my eyes but couldn't see a thing. It was really dark. All the lights were off.

What is going on?

Then, I heard a voice that said, "*Huwag kang maingay. Huwag kang sisigaw. Pag nagsumbong ka, papatayin kita.*" ("Don't make any noise, and don't even shout. If you tell anybody, I will kill you.")

What?

Who's that?

Where is this voice coming from?

Is someone beside me?

Oh no!

Arms were wrapped around my tiny body! I shook. I cried.

I begged, "*Para mo nang awa. Para mo nang awa. Umalis ka na. Oo, di ako magsusumbong. Umalis ka lang.*" ("Please leave. Please leave. Yes, I will not tell anyone. Just go.")

I felt like the world had ended. I didn't know what happened. I didn't know what was happening.

Please, Mother Mary, help me.

I begged some more and just couldn't stop crying. I will never forget that feeling. He got up and walked out of the room. Thank God! He turned the lights on, and I saw him in his underwear. It was my uncle! Not the businessman uncle, but one of my mother's brother! I locked the room, sat in the corner and cried the entire night. I went up to my bedside and got mad at my rosary and *Sto. Niño.*

Why did you let that happen?

Didn't I pray before I slept?

Don't I pray every day?

Why did you let him in?

Now what?

What do I do?

That was the longest, scariest night of my life. I couldn't wait to see the crack of dawn, so I could run away. I checked my body. I checked my underwear. I checked my clothes. I still had my little light orange jacket on. I still had my underwear on.

Am I bleeding?

Am I sore?

No, I guess nothing happened. I guess he just wrapped his arms around my body, that's all. But it didn't feel right.

Why would you do that to your niece?

I had so many questions and mixed emotions that night.

How dare you do that to me?

I was so mad! I cried for days and months! I prayed that I could forget. I wanted to stab him.

In my head I screamed, *"I will punch you in the face. I will hurt you. I hate you! Shame on you, devil!"*

I waited for the first light from the adjacent house. I went to tell my other uncle what his younger brother did to me that night. He listened, but that's it—he just listened. Maybe he believed me, maybe he didn't. I checked myself again, and I listened to my body. There were no bruises or bleeding. No pain. Nothing. Then, I came back to my rosary and *Sto. Niño* to say my thank you prayer. He didn't let it happen. He stopped him and woke me up. He protected me.

That almost broke me down.

At age 17, I was crushed.

My heart bled.

Do you want to know where my *Sto. Niño* is right now?

I still have it. It's in our bedroom in the house where I raised my five children. I still pray to my *Sto. Niño*. That is one of my treasured possessions, and I had it in my luggage when I migrated to the US in 2003.

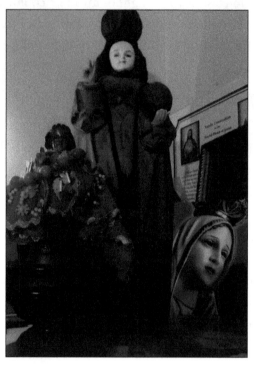

The red one is my college buddy, and the wooden *Sto. Niño* was a gift from my friend, Suzette Balgos.

Life is hard. It will pull you down if you let it get into your brain, but God is just so good. He was so good that he surprised me with a full scholarship for the second semester. I didn't tell my businessman uncle about it, so when he gave me money to pay for my second semester tuition, I took it and sent it to *Mamang*. I could have used it to buy myself some clothes, replace my "smiling shoes" (the soles folded down as I walked, making my shoes look like they were smiling), or buy hamburgers like what my friends in school did, but no, *Mamang* needed it more than I did. I figured she could use it to buy some sugar and milk for her instant coffee. My mom is a coffee drinker. We would roast rice over firewood and boil it to make coffee. Put a teaspoon of sugar, and voila! Freshly boiled rice coffee! It would be gourmet coffee if you had some evaporated milk or condensed milk as coffee creamer, but that didn't happen every day. We settled for boiled coffee with sugar as our regular. So when I got the scholarship money, I didn't think twice and gave it to *Mamang*. She deserved a good real instant coffee!

Someone liked me in school. He was the cousin of my best friend, Eppie Carlos. We dated, but it was a short relationship. It lasted for only two months, I think. We broke up... no, I lied! I got dumped (haha!) I guess I was just a boring girlfriend. I wanted to know what it was like to have a boyfriend, but it scared me because I didn't want to be distracted from my studies. I didn't want to end up like my brother, not finishing college, or like other girls I knew who needed to give up school because they got pregnant. I couldn't do that. I couldn't be that person. I needed to help my parents upgrade their lifestyle—that was my mission. I couldn't afford to go back home pregnant and sell fish in the market on Fridays. That breakup was the first time I felt a heartache, but it's ok, I accepted it. I wasn't attractive anyway, and to make matters worse, I was no fun!

Every day at school, I only had a few coins to spend for the day—just enough to buy *sago* (homemade sweet drink) and *hopia* (mung bread). My college friends hung out in the cafeteria and enjoyed their snacks while I acted like I wanted to spend time in the library, when the truth was I couldn't afford to buy what they were eating. They ate hamburgers or pizza while I went out and bought the cheaper snacks from street vendors outside the school campus. It was good and bad because after finishing my bite-sized *hopia,* I would just sit in the library and read magazine articles about family life and parenting. I knew I didn't have great parents, but I also knew we can't choose our parents. You just deal with it, and that's what I did. Having a bad experience in my own family, I was determined to not be like my parents if I became one. I made a commitment to myself that this kind of life stops with me. I knew I would be a good parent.

Every day at 6:00 p.m., after visiting the library, I attended mass. It refreshed me and kept me awake until the end of my classes. It strengthened me to face life's challenges. Besides, I was hungry and needed some nourishment (the Holy Communion) until my last class. Now, when my children whisper to my ear and tell me they are hungry during mass on Sundays, I tell them, "Don't worry, the Lord will feed you in Holy Communion (when we line up to receive the Body of Jesus), the way He fed me when I was in college." And they would roll their eyes because they think I'm not taking them seriously.

Before the week ends, I would prepare my mind and body for non-stop chores. I would hand-wash a week's worth of laundry. I wished I could spend a day doing my schoolwork and maybe relax a little, but that never happened. All day long I would be washing clothes, cooking, and cleaning their house. I was really worn out. Then my birthday came, but sadly no one knew. I didn't tell anybody, and they didn't care anyway. But I had the most memorable 18th birthday. I had manually washed heavy blankets and clothes all day. At the end of that day, I sat and looked at my bleeding hands, and hummed quietly to myself, "Happy birthday to me." It might be depressing for other people, but it wasn't for me because God and my Mother Mary were there for me, and I was thankful for my life.

Did any of my family members greet me?

No, we didn't have a phone.

Birthday card?

No, that was too expensive, but it's ok. I know they remembered my birthday.

After over a year, I felt something was wrong. My uncle, who I knew was a businessman, ran a business called ATIVAN GANG. One time, while I was cleaning their room, I saw a shoebox full of cash. It scared me. Then it became clear to me why he and his buddies came home past midnight and why he always had stacks of money. I later learned that his business was to lure foreigners to go out with his buddies and his beautiful female employees. They made the tourists buy stuff, then invite them to stay in a room, and finally they would drug them. They waited until they were out of their senses to rob them. They took their jewelry, cash, and who knows what else. I have nothing against my uncle. He was a good man, and he sent me to college. If not for him, I would still be in my town selling fish. He gave me a chance.

What wasn't right was what they did for a living. I didn't want to be a part of it. With modesty, I told him that I couldn't do the nanny job anymore.

Instead, I started working in my auntie's factory—the one who is married to an engineer and lived next door. After school, I got paid by the dozen to sew baby shoes and put pompoms on baby bonnets. It was just like what my mother did for a living when I was younger, except she had sewed in garters for shorts. I needed someone to help me pay for my food and *jeepney* (an open bus—it is the cheapest transportation available to majority of the Filipino people) fare for my daily commute, so I lived with my *Kuya* (brother) for a year. To save as much as possible, I walked half a mile with my umbrella in the hot midday sun to catch the *jeep*. Typically, people catch a tricycle to get to where the *jeepneys* are. If you see people walking in the sun with umbrellas on, I bet you, they're Asians. Yes! That's what Asians do.

One rainy night, I got off the *jeep* to an area that was usually busy with people sitting in front of their houses, just chatting or watching the world go by (again, that's typical of Filipinos). Normally, there would be kids playing on the street and *balut (duck eggs)* vendors calling out, but that night, the whole place was quiet. Nobody was out and the stores were closed. So I walked down the road with my umbrella. While walking, just minding my own business, I heard something from behind me. I looked back and saw a shadow with a lighted cigarette in his hand. I walked a little faster to increase my distance, but I heard his footsteps going faster as well. I remembered stories of girls being raped in the grassy open land down the road where it was dark. I ran, and he ran too. I ran faster, but he ran faster. My heart was pounding, and my brain started to think of what move I would do if he got me.

Oh, Lord! Please help me! I don't want to be raped. You want me to be a teacher! Yes, Lord! Save me from this evil one, so I can be a teacher.

I dropped my books, folders, and umbrella, kicked my shoes off, and ran faster than I've ever run before. Out of nowhere, a car with lights on came by and scared that guy away. Panting like a dog, I got into my brother's house, locked the door, and felt safe. That was the second scariest thing in my life.

That car that came by from nowhere?

I believe that was God's angel.

After that, my *Kuya* wouldn't let me walk alone at midnight. He would wake up and meet me where I get off the *jeep*. God bless the soul of my brother. He was my only brother. Sadly, he died of a heart attack in his early 40s. He was a good brother to me.

Meet my only brother, Kuya Ed. Due to lack of funds, *Mamang* made these white shorts out of some hand-me-down white pair of pants when I joined the Ms. Intramurals Contest to match my brother's. I put them on against my will.

At one point, I felt I was an inconvenience to my sister-in-law. They were having marital issues, and I didn't want to hear any of that. So I called my *Ate* (older sister), and she came to live with me in the house where I had the scariest and longest night of my life. I worked in a foreign-owned company that summer, and I met a Singaporean manager. I think I liked him, but I was too young for him. He was about 28 years old, and I was just 18. I really had a crush on him. In my junior year, I got letters from him. He seemed interested in me too and wished to meet my parents the next time he came over. He was waiting until I turned at least 20 years old.

Along the way, a guy who lived further down our street started eyeing me. He saw me one day when I was walking home with my *Kuya*. According to him, our P.E. classes shared the same pool one time, and he has had a crush on me ever since. He was glad to know that I lived in the same street. He lived with his sister and was taking Nautical Engineering, I think. To make the long story short, I started walking with him instead and to let *Kuya* enjoy his sleep after work. For the first time, I felt loved and cared for. He became my college boyfriend. He was good-looking, and even more so when he was in his uniform. It felt great to have someone take care of me. We would go to church together, he would pick me up from school (via *jeepney*), and we would go home together. He was a year older than me, which made me think he would graduate that year, but he didn't. I nagged and questioned him about it. I wanted to be with him for the rest of my life, but finishing a degree was and is very important to me (ask my five children about it.) I wanted us to be professionals if we were going to start a family. Well, he didn't graduate. Instead, he got a job in a hospital. He stopped seeing me and picking me up from school, and we didn't go to church together anymore like we used to. Then one day, my college friends and I went for a surprise visit at his work. There, we found out that he was dating one of the pretty nurses. I looked at myself in the mirror that night—between that sexy smooth-looking nurse and my pimply red sore face with jagged teeth, of course, he would pick the better choice. Between someone already in the work force and a student, of course, he'd pick her. I was hurt, broken, and saddened. I was dumped again. I had no luck in love.

In my junior year, I asked my *Mamang* to come and help me out. We worked as a team. She worked full time in my auntie's factory while I stayed in school for longer hours. By then, I was already working on my thesis writing. I needed more time to conduct surveys, collect data, and write up my study. We lived by the day. There was actually a bag of rice that had been sitting in that vacant house for years. We were hungry, so we took it even if it had some black specks already. I tried to get rid of the specks, but there were too many. We just cooked the rice and ate it. You know what I proved? Mouse poop is not poisonous. Yup! True story.

We made ends meet. But hardworking as she has always been, she would pick up extra hours and iron other people's clothes after working all day. She ironed the clothes of my auntie and cousins. She had mountains of clothes to press on their front porch. I was worried and told her she didn't have to do that because I did some sewing at night anyway. One night, I saw her on the porch and heard her coughing while ironing their clothes. It was 11:30 p.m., almost midnight, but she was still working.

Did they even care to feed her or offer a cup of coffee to keep her awake?

No!

How could you do that to your own sister?

I wanted to tell my auntie, "Your sister came to the city to help her daughter finish college, and we both work hard to make it through. I get that you pay for her service, but come on! She hasn't had dinner yet. Don't you have extra food to spare for your own sister?"

I went straight to that house, went in, walked across their living room (in front of them watching their TV show), grabbed my mother's arm, and brought her to our place. I cried and got so mad at my auntie in silence because she was maltreating my *Mamang,* who happens to be her sister. With that, I promised my *Mamang* that I will do everything to help her out after I graduate.

In my senior year, my schedule changed. My school requirements became more demanding and required me to be more available in school. I did my practice teaching all morning and attended my classes in the afternoon. I had to call *Ate* to come and stay with me for a year, so I could finish my degree. *Mamang* went back to our little town. I was a full-time student throughout the day, and I worked during the night. I continued to do my sewing job after school. On weekends, I would make ice candies and cook dishes to sell to my auntie's employees. They worked six days a week and had two breaks during the day. One was at 10 a.m. and the other at 3 p.m. In between those times, I would make things up to sell, so I could have some money to spend for my projects. I really didn't have time to sit down and study for my tests or work on my projects and thesis at home. I did everything while in school, so I could just concentrate on sewing at night. Thank

God we survived that last year. I was very excited to graduate. I was eager to earn real money, so I could finally help my family. We were getting ready for graduation. I saved some money, so I could buy a nice graduation dress and have my hair fixed for the graduation picture.

But guess what?

It was a disaster!

I thought I would look pretty after my hair and makeup, but I looked like a witch!

What in the world happened to my hair?

Don't they understand that this is very monumental to me? I paid someone to make me look pretty, not ugly!

I was very disappointed.

The most horrific yearbook picture in 1990 and my normal face on graduation day.

Well, like what people always say, "Life goes on."

Before graduation, I thought I'd give my heart another try. I wanted to share my joy to the boy who loved me before meeting that cute nurse. I tried to reach out to him but to no avail. He was already set to that girl. I was broken again—totally dumped. So I walked across the stage to get my college diploma sniffling and very sad because I didn't have anybody to share my joy and accomplishments with. My parents were also not there to see me graduate. I couldn't deny though that their absence made me appreciate them even more because each one played a major part and contributed to my college education. I wouldn't be where I am right now if not for them. My graduation was a product of teamwork and hard work from everyone in my family. I felt a heavy cross was set on my shoulder as a young adult but was hopeful that my sorrows were about to end the moment I finish my degree.

I had a very sad life.

Am I complaining?

No, I was just stating a fact.

Was I grateful?

Yes, because that meant I would not sell fish in the market or plant rice in the field anymore.

Was I appreciative?

Yes, I appreciate my life.

Going through all those hardships made me a stronger person. At least I wouldn't get sunburnt like the people in my town.

Was my face clear?

No, it was still full of pimples with ripe acnes.

It's alright. Life is good. Well, God was there for me since day one. Though crushed and broken, I knew there was a brighter future ahead of me. Three months before I graduated, I was recommended, interviewed, and then offered a position as a teacher in one of the prestigious schools in my country. There was a new job waiting for me. This meant new life, new beginning, and a new environment. With that in mind, I thought that was the end of my sorrowful experiences.

But I was wrong. I got nailed and crucified to a bad marriage.

5

CHAPTER

My Failed Marriage

B efore graduating at the age of 20, I got a job offer as a pre-kindergarten teacher at De La Salle Santiago-Zobel School, my first real job. A big thanks to my professor for giving me a glowing recommendation. After all the days of hard work to survive college and to make ends meet, I got my Bachelor of Science in Elementary Education Degree, Major in Reading, and graduated Cum Laude. All those sleepless nights and tears were worth it because now, I am finally done.

Or so I thought.

It was May 1990, my first day of work. All the teachers and staff were in the auditorium for the assembly to welcome the veteran teachers and to introduce the newbies. It was time to introduce the new teachers, and I was one of them! I wore a light green plain top which I bought from the city market. It was a decent blouse. In fact, I had it on when I graduated because it was my fanciest blouse thus far. Then I matched it with a pleated skirt that *Mamang* sewed for me. She found this checkered fabric and thought it would be a nice pattern for my skirt. So I had that matching outfit and waited confidently for my name to be called. With my bright pimply faced, fresh-grad smile, I looked around to see my co-workers. The guy beside me was nice, and we made small talk that made me feel comfortable. Then I heard my name. I got up, raising my hand a little to be recognized. I felt confident. My new clothes made me feel good. Didn't I mention in the previous chapter that confidence is like an outfit? You have to wear it! I wore that confidence. Well, the nice guy beside me leaned over to whisper something to my ear after I was introduced. I thought he had found me cute. I thought he would say I looked pretty in my outfit. So I leaned towards him to wait for what he was about to say.

With modesty, he said, "Have you seen the students' uniform yet?"

"No, why?" I replied.

He answered, "The girls' uniform doesn't exactly look like your skirt, but it is close enough. You might consider NOT wearing that on a school day."

My confidence level?

Gone!

Flushed down the toilet in an instant.

Oh, dear God! Why am I always unlucky with clothes?

Now, my first day in my first job for the new school year was ruined. But God never ceases to pick me up whenever I'm at my lowest point. The next thing I know, some ladies came by to take our measurements. I couldn't believe it! We were going to get uniforms for regular days and a set of gala uniform with the school's logo on it for special days. How great is our God? Truly, an amazing God! I just needed to shop for new shoes when I receive my first pay.

My first teaching year was a bit challenging. Since I had done my practice teaching with upper grades (3-6), I never knew what it was like to be in a Pre-K class.

Why am I teaching this age group?

I was clueless; I didn't know what to do with snotty kids. So I looked around, observed my co-workers, and learned from them. Before I knew it, I was a happy Pre-K teacher! Thank you so much to my former Prep co-workers, who became my extended family. *Salamat* Suzette, Ditas, Baby, Boots, Lucy P., Chie A., Sally, Nina, and Joji Castillo (may she rest in peace.) The first school year went by pretty quickly. The guy who sat next to me during that unforgettable orientation day inspired me. He was nice. We talked and laughed. We shared stories and laughed again. I always looked forward to seeing him at faculty meetings. He was a good guy, but he was not a Catholic. I like Catholic dudes because I want to go to church with someone. I want God to see how I share my faith with my special someone. That was my fantasy. Ultimately, nothing came out of our interactions, which only consisted of waving at each other in the hallway and sitting next to each other during meetings. My heart beat faster when I saw him, but that was all. Besides, who would date a girl who wears a school uniform to work? Nope! Not him!

Fast forward to my second year of teaching. We were back at the auditorium for another assembly to welcome the new members of the staff. A new teacher, an ex-seminarian was one of them. Oh, wow! That was so Catholic! However, he's not my type. He is 5'2", and I am 5'6". Just in physical terms, we were not a good pair at all. He would always sit next to me when I wanted to sit next to the guy I first met, the one who makes me laugh. I like being around him, not this new teacher. He would always ask me questions, and since I was an older teacher, I just had to help him. I showed him around and gave him tips and suggestions on how the school ran. That's all I wanted to do, but he would always follow me around.

Surprisingly, we rode on the same bus. By the way, the school lets teachers and staff ride the school bus with the students. We get off at a hub to help us save some commuting money. That was just one of the teacher benefits from my school. From the hub, we would go on our separate ways depending on where we lived. This guy, the new guy, was like a shadow. He wouldn't leave me alone. So I figured, I could match him with my cousin, for they have the same height. But to make the story short, he was after me, not my cousin. Sometimes, I would hide and hope that my bus would leave before he could hop in. He could catch the second bus anyway. Every day, I prayed he would miss the bus I would ride. Finally, after less than a year of avoiding him, I thought it would be okay if I gave him a chance. Naïvely, I thought that since he was a Catholic and an ex-seminarian, he must be holy. He spent his high school and college years in the seminary, so that met my criteria. Alrighty!

We started dating and planned on getting married the following year. Before the wedding, we fought and argued. We just didn't get along. He would always force me to do things against my will. He was also very lustful, and I didn't like it. I broke up with him, but after seeing him cry, I felt bad. I didn't want to hurt anybody. That was the last thing that I wanted to do, to be the cause of someone's grief.

Alright... alright... I thought to myself, *let's try again.*

Wedding plans were still in place. We went shopping for giveaways and my wedding dress. By the way, wedding dresses are such a big thing for brides. You pick your style, and they'll make sure it fits perfectly on your body. Some have it tailored, but my wedding dress? It was just one of those displayed in the market, nothing fancy. I don't wear fancy clothes anyway. In fact, most of my clothes are still hand-me-downs. I am not picky at all. For people who know me, we can play a little guessing game with my outfit. When you see me, look over my clothes and figure out where I got it from. This is a multiple-choice type of test:

A. Hand-me-downs

B. Goodwill/thrift Store

C. Yard Sale

D. Clearance rack at the store

E. All of the above

If your answer is right, I pray you get more blessings from the heavens! You can't say no to that!

Well, we argued and fought throughout the whole wedding process. One time, we were out shopping, and we got into a big fight. I don't remember what we were fighting about. I walked away and got on a *jeepney*. He chased me and pulled me out of that vehicle.

I thought, "Really? You did that? We are not even married yet!"

Two months before the wedding day, I got pregnant. Yes, I was two months pregnant with my Child #1 before I got married. I wasn't very happy because I felt that marrying this guy was not right. The flowers were set. The church was set. My parents were set to arrive in Manila. Wedding entourage was all set. I already met his parents and family, and I liked them. But despite all this, there was something in this man that made me not want to walk down the aisle. The night before I put that cheap dress on, I stood still. I didn't want to touch my gown. I didn't feel like wearing it, but I was pregnant, and everything was ready for the next day. I didn't tell anybody what I felt, not even my own mother. If I said something, I might just get yelled at.

I didn't want to hear words like, *we did this... we bought that... we spent money on this and that. You wasted our time. What will other people think? What will the people in our town say? Blah... blah... blah.*

I went to confession. No one knew my apprehensions except Mother Mary and my God. I walked down the aisle the following day, put a smile on my face, and looked around and hoped that things will be ok.

The day after our wedding, we moved to our little house somewhere south. It was a low-cost housing. He got a house somewhere in Laguna, more than an hour away from where we taught. I tried to live a normal life as a wife and a future mother. Meanwhile, he still did what he loved doing: Karate. One time, I went to see him compete. He fought against someone taller than him. It was a tough fight, but it ended well. He won a trophy for being the Black Belt Champion. Yes, this young wife was proud of him. To my surprise, he was talking to some pretty ladies with his trophy in his hand but never introduced me as his wife. I thought I looked cute when I was pregnant, and I wore my red sleeveless dress. I thought he would be proud of me but nope! My feelings were a little hurt, and I think I asked him why he didn't mention something about having a wife, but I couldn't recall what he said.

I actually want to remember what he said, but I really can't.

On Sundays, we would regularly go to church in Canlubang, Laguna to attend the mass. In fairness, he introduced me one time to his former mentor and classmates. That felt good. While he talked to his seminarian friends, I walked around the church premises. I still remember when I picked a young guava fruit and ate it. I prayed that the baby in my womb will be blessed as I ate that fruit that grew from a holy place. I tried to juggle adjusting to married life, figuring out how to be a parent to my first born, and getting to know the father of my baby. We didn't really know each other yet as we got married too soon. Well, my belly popped that summer of 1993. I was 23 years old when I became a mother to my Child #1. He was named **Duval Nique** because his father's name means **"valley"** and Duval means "from the valley." We threw in Nique because he was born on August 27, the Feast Day of St. Mo**nique.**

I wasn't ready to be a mother then, but I was very excited to see my newborn baby. His father came up to me when I woke up and he said, "He's ugly." Still high from my epidural and seeing everything as foggy, I got up and walked down the nursery. I looked for my child and whispered to myself, "He was right. My baby looks like an old man."

Did it have something to do with our regular fighting? Was he frowning the whole time he was in my belly?

Oh, no! Poor child!

This new young unprepared mother just had an ugly-looking baby boy. His eyes were slits, and his face wasn't moist—it was dry and crinkled.

Well, I was recovering from my delivery, and I needed rest. When I returned to the room, guess who was asleep on my hospital bed?

My husband!

What in the world?

In my head, I wondered, "Why can't he sleep on the chair, or perhaps just go home and leave me alone? He doesn't take care of me anyway. I was the one in labor for hours, so don't I deserve the whole bed?"

No, he shared the bed with me because he said he couldn't get a good rest on the chair. Oh well, alright. I'll share some space.

A few weeks after I gave birth, my parents came to assist us with the baby. Having a child is no joke! You, young people out there, I tell you... you have to be mentally, physically, emotionally, and financially ready before you decide to have one. In my case, I didn't have the chance to think and prepare in any way. It just happened right in front of me. I was forced to be ready and strong for my baby.

To give you an idea of what it was like in my tiny house, picture this: box-studio type with a sink and a bathroom. That's all. No oven, no dishwasher, no washing machine, and no laundry room, but we did have a queen-sized mattress (which occupied almost the entire house), a refrigerator, a 14-inch TV, and a couch. That red 14-inch TV was purchased from my first pay-check from my first job. Remember when I used to walk and watch TV from the window when I was a kid, and they closed their window while I was watching? I told myself that one day... one day... I would buy my own TV and never have to go to other people's house to see my favorite variety show. Yep! I made it happen. Well, we just had the basics in our starter home. It's better than the "Spiderman house" back home, right?

Anyway, during the day, I used cloth diapers for Baby #1. I put Pampers on him at night and waited until it got jello-looking before I changed him. The diaper should be heavily soaked before it went to the trash as I needed to get my money's worth. During the daytime, I would put him in a folding bed when he slept, so when he peed in his diaper cloth, the pee streamed freely through the bed. I didn't want to wake the baby up just to change his diaper. He was a little wet, but not soggy. When he woke up, he had flooded the floor. You know how moms take the opportunity to start doing all the work when babies sleep? Yes, I did that! I wanted to do everything that I could do while he slept. I would do the laundry, clean up the house, and wash/sterilize the feeding bottles. By the way, I boiled the bottles as we had no fancy sterilizer.

One time, my hands were full, very full. There was pee on the floor, so I asked the father to dry it since he wasn't doing anything anyway. My parents were fixing the yard at the back, so he was the only one that could help. Unexpectedly, he got upset with me. I got upset too, since I was tired doing all the work in the house.

What's the big deal with cleaning up the floor? Besides, that's his child right there!

He yelled at me, and I yelled back at him. We fought. He grabbed my hair.

I got so mad because he did that with my parents around. I was like, "Seriously?" Could he not at least fake it for my parents? I felt embarrassed and degraded. I was mad because he had the nerve to show off his ugly behavior to my parents. My parents were shocked at what they saw. They expressed their frustration but tried not to intervene because they knew that if they did, it was not going to end well. They just left with a heavy heart.

I thought about what he did. I still couldn't believe he did that to me! I just gave birth and was still recovering. My gut told me I needed to be prepared for something worse. If he can do this to me now, what else can he do? I felt the need to be secure and to have a Plan B in case this marriage doesn't last. Can you imagine feeling scared within the first year of marriage? That was so bad, right? Anyway, when Nique was only months old, I went to the Phase II office, the site where houses have a bigger floor area. I inquired about getting a new house under my name. I got one and rented it out while we stayed in the first house. Meanwhile, we added two rooms and extended the kitchen in the first house because we needed some space. It was a pretty decent house for a starter.

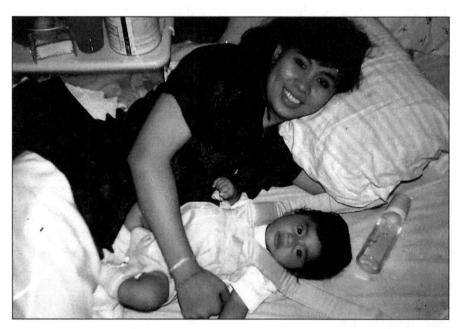

My first heart at about 3 months old.

Thankfully, Child #1 turned out to be a cute chunky baby. Life went on. My husband and I worked in the same school. He taught science in the grade school building while I was a Pre-K teacher in the pre-school building. Some facts about him: he was a Science Major, artistic, and a good-looking teacher. No wonder, there were some teachers who I think had a crush on him.

Every summer, before school starts, our school would hold an institutional field trip. When I say, "field trip," I mean a real field trip that took days! We dropped off Nique to his grandma's house so that we could go. That was very hard for me because I always slept beside my baby boy. It was our first night away from each other, and I cried when I left him. We went to *Palawan*, a beautiful island and a tourist spot in the southern part of the country. We travelled by water going there and flew back. By the way, this was all paid for by my school. The school administration really takes care of their staff. They value what we do, so missing a treat like this is unheard of. Anyway, everybody was having a good time with food, fellowship, and festivities. We went to the underground river via boat, and we needed to hop out of the boat because it couldn't get any closer to the shore. That meant we were going to have to get wet from waist down. It was ok for most of us as we were there to get wet anyway. I got off with the older teachers while he stayed with the younger teachers. Then someone called my attention to check and look at my husband behind us.

Guess what I saw?

My husband, carrying the young teacher who had a crush on him. He carried her in his arms all the way to the shore.

What did all the other teachers think?

Everyone was just talking about the scene the entire time. It was like a blockbuster movie called *Pakarga* (Carry Me), which everyone joked about to break the ice. My vacation, which just started, was ruined—totally ruined! I tried to put on a fake smile until the end of the day, but I confronted him when we were in the room. Imagine how hard it is to control your voice when you are so mad. I didn't want the people next door to hear us fighting. I whispered in anger! Whispered with tears in my eyes. Whispered in pain.

I was so embarrassed by his actions. I whispered in silence how he ended what I thought would be a grand vacation for me.

What in the world is this man doing?

Flirting?

Flirting in front of everybody?

My first vacation night in that beautiful place was a sleepless night. I cried my feelings away all through the night. I wished I could punch him in the face! I prayed for self-control. I prayed that God would help me understand the things that I didn't understand. To give me the courage to face my co-workers and act like everything was fine.

The next day, at breakfast, I put on my sunglasses to cover my swollen eyes. The older teachers hugged me, and they made me feel a little better. A big thank you to them as well. I still remember clearly the warmth of Zeny Coronel's tight hug. For the rest of the trip, I just didn't want to talk to my "famous" husband. I didn't want to be around him. I just avoided him. Finally, it was time to fly back. I was glad to have my baby boy in my arms again. I wished I had just stayed with my child and had not seen what I saw. I could have been in a better state of mind if I stayed, but we can't turn back time. It happened. I just needed to deal with it. So, what now, Lord?

Did I say he was a science teacher?

Yes, he was.

He could have been a good science teacher, but he didn't keep up with the requirements of being one. He didn't make lesson plans, didn't grade the test papers on time, and didn't submit grades by the due date. In short, he was holding everybody up in his team. The homeroom teachers cannot send the report cards without the science grade. Again, we would argue. I started questioning his priorities and sense of responsibility. He spent so much time watching TV and working on his projects that had been "in progress" at home.

Another fact about him is he is a handyman. He would work on his metal cabinet, which was great, but God forgive me if I lost my patience. His tools, nails, screws, and metal pieces were always on the floor. With a small baby starting to walk and chewing on things, it was not safe at all! Don't forget, my dear readers, we lived in a very small house. Those tools and other building materials were just lying under the dining table.

Who in their right mind does that?

Who would have patience with that?

How long does it take to finish making that freaking cabinet?

Evidently, more than a year! At some point, I got tired of nagging and just ignored it—I ignored it completely. I just shoved everything in his corner and trained little Nique NOT to go to that forbidden place. I think I did a great job with my son. He didn't put any screws in his mouth or walk through those metal pieces. Even this child learned to be flexible at a very young age. I love to clean the house whenever I get the chance, so imagine my frustration when I could clean everything except that part of the house. That corner literally turned gray. It's no joke! Thick layers of dust had turned that spot gray.

As the song from movie "Frozen" says, "Let it go." So, I let go. Why worry so much about something I cannot change? As time went on, his problem in school remained. He was always late with turning grades in.

I questioned him. "How busy are you that you don't have time to check your students' test papers?"

I knew what it was like to be a teacher because I was and still is a teacher myself. But I always got the work done. He didn't.

Did he do what I did at home?

Did he cook?

Did he clean the house?

Did he do the laundry? (Sometimes)

Did he wash the dishes? (He thinks it's a woman's job.)

Did he take care of the baby the way I did?

Again, Lord Jesus, please strengthen me and bless me with **MORE PATIENCE!**

I paused, took a deep breath, and started helping him grade his test papers. We would sit across the table and check the papers quietly. He has barely finished a class, and the next thing I know, he's already snoring! I spent hours grading his test papers to get the work done.

Who ends up checking ALL the papers, then?

Me! I do it so that the only thing left for him to do is to enter the grades.

Is it fair for me to do his work?

I'd say, it's *ok*.

Besides, we are husband and wife.

I am expected to support and help him.

"In sickness and in health, 'till death do us part."

I get it.

He solved his problem by transferring to the Physical Education Department, which meant no lesson plans to make, and no test papers to grade. He came up with a performance-based grade. He was having fun. He liked it. He was having so much fun as a PE teacher that he forgot to take care of his pregnant wife. Every day, we would fight. There was not a day that we did not argue when I was pregnant with Child #2.

Yep!

I got pregnant again after three and a half years.

We had been married for five years, but you may be asking, "Are you sure? How did it happen?"

I refuse to recall.

He would come home late—very late—but I would stay up to wait for him. I would sometimes do the laundry to keep myself awake. Doing laundry back home was not as easy as we do it here in the US. I only had a washer that only spun the clothes with soap. I needed to fill it up with water using a hose. After spinning, I still needed to pick the clothes up one by one, wring it, and rinse manually. Then, drain the washer manually for the next load. I would line up three basins of water for the rinsing process. Since there was no dryer, I needed to hang them one by one on a clothesline. When he came home, he would say he was tired and didn't want to be bothered. Oh well, I'll just finish all the laundry. At least he was still alive.

Yes, I would do the laundry past midnight if I had to.

It came to a point where I didn't even want to see his face. I didn't want to be anywhere near him. I wanted to do something that would free me of his presence.

Should I tutor on Saturdays?

That would mean I had to commute and travel from one house to another. But I couldn't drive. I had never driven a car back home. I only learned to drive when I came to the US when I was already 36 years old.

I thought to myself, *Should I start my master's degree at De La Salle University? It's free anyway!*

However, this would mean I had to commute for about two hours, which would cost me some money, but at least I didn't have to see him for a day.

It would be nice to have a stress-free day!

But I wasn't sure if I had time to study and do homework during the week. I taught full-time, tutored after school, and took care of baby Nique at home. I hesitated, but our Department Head came up to me one morning and handed me my class schedule for my master's degree. I don't remember her exact words, but she said something to this effect, "Here! This is your schedule, and you start this coming Saturday. Be there on time!"

Shocking but exciting, huh?

I'll be by myself for one full day! That was in 1996. I remember smiling again.

Whoa!

That was liberating!

Guess what?

I couldn't avoid him completely. I was only free on Saturdays.

We worked at the same place, so I had to ride in the car with him to save money. Besides, if I used public transportation, it would cost me a lot more, so I had no choice.

Just get in the car and deal with him for a little over an hour while he drives to work.

Those were the words I had to tell myself every day.

When I was pregnant with Child #2, I was always upset. It is so hard to pretend you're happy when you're not. You know the feeling when your blood is boiling? To make matters worse, when you're pregnant, your emotions are quite unpredictable. I was emotional and sensitive, but he didn't care. He didn't think about what I felt.

One night, we had a big fight, again. I really don't remember what we were fighting about. We had so many fights that I can't remember the details anymore. Every day, we fought and argued about things—some were serious, some were petty. We just don't get along! Anyway, I think I was nagging about how I needed help at home. I needed him to do more chores at home since my belly was getting bigger, and it was hard for me to do all the work while taking care of Nique. We fought intensely the next morning on our way to work and fought even more on our way back home. Instead of talking in the car, we just fought! I think I was seven or eight months pregnant at that time. We got home, and I was in the room with Nique. I put him to bed then I tried to sleep, but I couldn't. Something was hurting. I tossed and turned a couple of times. Then, I felt contractions. I was bleeding. I went out of the room and told him I was bleeding, and I needed to see the doctor. He was watching TV when I told him.

Did he even move?

Did he show concern?

Did he worry about my condition?

Did he think it was an emergency?

Did he think I might lose the baby?

NO!

He was a jerk!

A jerk!

A jerk!

A jerk!

I wished I knew how to drive. I wished there was someone other than him that I could ask to bring me to the hospital. I checked the time. It was 1 a.m., which meant there would be no available tricycles outside (a tricycle is what I needed to get out of the subdivision, to get to the *jeepney*, which would take me to the hospital). I asked this jerk again to drive me to the hospital because I was bleeding and couldn't commute on my own past midnight.

You may ask, "Why didn't you call 911?"

Oh, I don't think there was such a thing at my place. I know... third world country. Save your own life!

Why didn't I call my parents?

They were on the island which was nine hours away from me.

How about his parents?

They were two hours away and didn't have a car at that time.

Imagine what this young pregnant bleeding lady looked like in front of the young husband watching TV on the couch. In the end, he didn't get the key. He didn't drive. He didn't bring me to the hospital.

Why?

Because he was mad at me.

Because he wanted me to apologize to him first and said I should beg before he could bring me to the hospital.

WHAT A HUGE JERK!

I yelled and bled even more from frustration. I wanted to smack his face!

Seriously? This is what you're thinking now? This is what you want me to do right now? Oh, God! What did I get myself into with this man? Why do I need to beg? Why do I need to apologize? For what? Asking you to help me do the chores in the house? Isn't life more important? There are two lives in danger here! Don't you know that?

I looked at Nique sleeping peacefully, then, I turned to my small altar.

I stopped yelling.

I stopped getting mad.

I stopped getting upset.

Instead, I sobbed and prayed.

I prayed and sobbed and begged Mother Mary to please help me keep my unborn baby safe.

I held my tummy and asked for a miracle. There was nothing I could do at that moment. There was no one else to turn to. I knew she understood what I felt because like me, she is a mother. I was scared... really, really scared. I didn't want to lose my baby. I wasn't ready for this baby, but I will do anything and everything to keep my children.

He was still watching TV. I prayed then I fell asleep. I woke up the next day and felt so much better. When I went for my regular checkup, the doctor said everything was fine. Thank God! I believe my prayers were answered. Keep your faith, and you will be surprised how God works in your life. I thank Mama Mary for her intervention. I believe in miracles.

Baby #2 was born. She was named **Gene Louise Kimberly**, and nicknamed Micci. Yes, she has a very long name, don't judge me. She has three first names because I thought she would be my last child. I wanted to give her all the names that I would want for a girl. "Gene" because she was born on the Feast Day of St. **Gene**vieve, January 3rd. "Kimberly" because I fell in love with that name when I saw it in a box, and Louise just because it gives a nice ring when you put <u>Gene Louise Kimberly</u> together. I am glad she was smart enough to memorize and write her full name before she attended Pre-K.

One of the parents of my students in De La Salle Santiago-Zobel, the school where I taught, was a gynecologist. God is so good! She delivered my two children free of charge! God always makes our ends meet. Thank you,

Dr. Medina Malit! After a hard labor, I pooped the baby out. After all the tears and blood while I had her in my womb, she came out perfect. She was a beautiful baby, but the most fretful of all. She wore me out! Every day was a long day. Every night was an almost sleepless night. I would be so lucky to have just three hours of uninterrupted sleep. I needed to keep an eye on her especially at night because for some reason, after feeding, she would throw up like a fountain. Yes! It was weird! So when it happened, it fell back on her face and got into her nose, making her unable to breathe. By the way, my children always slept with me.

The father?

Oh, he slept on the couch. We never slept together on the bed.

How did I get pregnant then?

I'll tell you later.

One night, after feeding baby Micci, I fell asleep. Then, she threw up while I was asleep. Mind you, when I sleep, I really sleep. If I could wish something from Santa on Christmas, it would be to sleep. Sleep for the whole week! But I was awakened by some movement beside me. I opened my eyes, and I saw baby Micci's face covered with *suka* (vomit). She was shaking and she couldn't breathe. Her nose was clogged up.

Oh, dear God!

Oh dear, Mama Mary!

What do I do?

I blamed myself for sleeping.

Her skin turned blue. I didn't know what to do. Do I need to remind you again? Calling 911 was foreign to me. I still couldn't drive at that time. I was in panic. I woke Nique up. I told him about his sister. I instructed him to sit up and help me pray. He opened his eyes and sat up but fell back asleep on the bed. Oh, boy! What do you expect from a kid? *Ok, I'll just let you sleep.* I looked at the father sleeping on the couch. Forget it! We might end up fighting again. I couldn't afford to argue this time. I needed help. I needed someone to help me pray for this baby.

Guess what?

I found no one.

I stood at the same altar I stood at when I almost lost her. I looked at the statue of Jesus and Mary, and said, "You protected this baby in my womb. You gave this baby to me, Lord Jesus. Are you going to take her back?"

I cried and cried.

What will I do?

I don't want to lose this baby, but it looks like she's not going to make it.

I looked at her one last time and held her up close to my chest. I offered her to God. I couldn't do anything except wait for the next thing to happen. She was motionless. I thought she was gone. I prayed the rosary. Then, all of a sudden, baby Micci sneezed and smiled at me!

Oh, thank God!

Oh, thank you Mama Mary!

I cried and cried so hard after that.

Miracles always do happen.

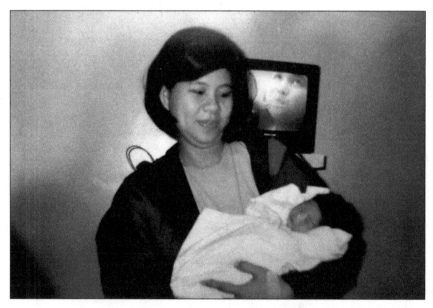

My second heart is one day old.

*****

Moving along, and as the kids were growing, my life as a mother of two kids was now a lot busier than before. On top of that, working full-time as a Pre-K teacher and a private tutor after school was tough. I could hardly find time to breathe. I forgot to take care of myself. I would take a shower and put on a clean uniform, but that was about it. At least I washed my hair with real shampoo and conditioner—not the laundry bar soap that I used when I was younger.

Have you seen the Pantene shampoo and conditioner that come in packets?

That's my kind of shampoo. I couldn't even afford to buy shampoo in bottles. Once the pack was empty, I put some water in it and dipped my forefinger in to get all its contents. That would be my last use before tossing it in the trash. The same goes with toothpaste. When the tube was almost out, I put it on a flat surface, and run something on top of the tube to push all the toothpaste to its end. That would serve me for at least another week. When it was empty, I would cut the tube in half, dip my toothbrush in and roll it all around. It would then last for about two more days. Only then could I toss my toothpaste tube in the trash.

Bye, bye!

So, looking at the bright side, at least I could still wash my hair and brush my teeth despite my very busy schedule.

In the Philippines, it is normal to have a stay-in babysitter called a *yaya*. They become a part of the household, like a family. Parents work all day while the *yayas* take care of the children and do all the house chores. They eat what we eat, and we go to church together. *Yayas* are paid monthly. You may ask how we find them. We can get them from anywhere, actually. We talk to people from work, friends, neighbors, and families from the province and ask for recommendations. With me having two kids, I needed two *yayas*. One was in charge of the kids, and the other would do the housework. Our combined pay barely made the bills. My priority was to keep the *yayas* as long as possible. I treated them well because I knew what it felt like to be treated badly. It happened to me when I was in college, remember? I had no intentions of doing the same thing to my children's *yayas*. Another reason to treat them well was the fact that my children's safety and well-being depended on them while I was gone for work. My mother-in-law, who had been very supportive of us, helped us find a *yaya* from her province who was about my age. My parents found another one from our province, and she was an elderly woman. I thought it was a perfect blend: the older lady could be in charge of my children while the younger one could take care of the laundry, cook, clean, and do the other house chores. After work, however, I took over. I played with the kiddos. I fed them and "home-schooled" them. Before they even attended school, they were academically ready. Their fine motor skills were well-developed. They could write their names nicely and neatly between three lines at age 4. Most importantly, I made sure they had good manners before entering school. That's just the teacher in me.

Things in our house were running pretty smoothly, and everyone seemed to be doing what was expected. The dusty, gray corner in our house finally cleared up. Thank you, Jesus! Then, one day, the older lady (God bless her soul) needed to go back home because her husband got sick. She was gone for a few months, so that became a problem. I needed to find another *yaya* from somewhere, but I didn't know where that somewhere would be. Thankfully, the younger *yaya* said she was fine to be alone. Instead of getting a new person, I would just pay her more to do extra work. I asked her to prioritize the kids—just cook and feed them on weekdays. On weekends, she could do whatever it was that she needed to do around the house while I took care of the kids and did some cooking and cleaning.

Agreed!

I thanked her for working with me. She was such a hardworking lady. On some nights when I stayed up late to cook for the next day, I would see her take a shower and iron clothes at around 11:30 p.m.

So hardworking, right?

Our house at that time had two rooms. One room was bigger, and it had a door. That was where my children and I slept. The other one was for the *yayas*. We ran out of budget when we did the extension, so it didn't have a door. Every night, before I went to bed, I would see her iron our clothes in her room.

In my head I'd say, *Wow! You really want to finish all your work, huh? Ok! Goodnight. I have to get some sleep and be ready for work the next morning. But girl, go to sleep! It's almost midnight. You can do that on weekends.*

Well, I would just say "goodnight." The kids were sleeping, and I was done with my chores, so I went to bed with my Nique and Micci.

Life went smoothly.

No problem.

Thank God!

Sometimes, I would get up at dawn to get some stuff ready for the next workday. Coming from our room, I would always see my children's father sleeping on the couch wearing his loose shorts, without brief or boxers. His private parts were showing. I told him, "Have you lost your mind? Do you realize that there's another person in this house? Do you not want to look decent at night? The *yaya* might see you like this! She stays up late, remember? What if she sees you looking like this? Have some shame in yourself!" Well, my words just fell on deaf ears.

Nique loved watching Mickey Mouse; he used to watch his VHS tapes over and over. I doze off easily when I watch TV, so I taught Nique how to turn off the VHS player and TV in case I fell asleep. I still fall asleep like this.

What? I grew up without TV, remember? So, I'm not used to watching TV for hours. My eyes easily get tired. When I stop to sit, that means I'll see you tomorrow. Nique watches TV, but the TV watches me... all the time. On some days when I cleaned the house, I would see VHS tapes that I hadn't seen before (Remember VHS tapes in the 90s? Our technology has improved a lot since then.) I was confused because the only tapes my kids played were Disney ones, especially Mickey Mouse. One day, I plugged in one of the unknown tapes.

Horrifying!

It was porn!

What?

I panicked!

What if Nique sees those nasty tapes?

What if he plays them by accident?

This father is just so irresponsible!

I was furious!

But I asked Nique gently, *"Kuya Nique, sinubukan mo ba i-play itong mga to?"* (Kuya Nique, did you ever try watching these tapes?)

I pointed at them.

He replied, "Hindi po, Mama." (No, Mama.)

He only liked Mickey Mouse.

I sighed a deep sigh of relief.

I told Nique and Micci to play outside. Then I confronted the father. My blood was boiling! I remember saying, "You know, what? I don't care what you watch, but please put your stuff away before everybody wakes up. We have two innocent kids in this house so, please, please, be mindful!"

Then, one time I got up early, and I went to the kitchen. From the kitchen, I saw our *yaya* get up and put on her underwear. I pretended I didn't see anything.

She said, "Good morning."

And I said, "Good morning," back.

But in my head, I thought, *Wow! You sleep without underwear? I wonder what it feels like, because I haven't done it.*

Oh well, not my business, I guess.

One Sunday morning, Micci was scheduled to get a shot at a clinic which was an hour away from home. On top of that, the doctor's office was always busy, especially on weekends. So I thought it was smart to have something ready for lunch when we came home after the checkup. I asked our hardworking *yaya* to go buy the ingredients to make *sinigang na baboy.*

(pork in sour soup). I took a shower and packed the kids' stuff. While the *yaya* was gone, a voice inside of me told me to go to the *yaya's* room. I never checked our *yaya's* stuff—I haven't even gone to their room. They may go to my room, but I don't go to theirs. I don't know why; it's just being me. I ignored the voice. I wanted us to hit the road and be the first in line at the doctor's office. We were ready to go. The kids and their father were in the car. I went back inside to use the restroom. The voice was still calling me, and there was some energy that I couldn't describe that was pulling me towards the *yaya's* room.

Alright, alright!

Let me do it then.

I sat on her bed. Looked left and right. Looked under the bed. Then the small table beside her bed caught my eye. On it was a blue small notebook. I wondered...

What's in this notebook?

Maybe a list of things that she wants to buy.

Or debts that she owes, or some important stuff.

Slowly, I pulled it and opened it. I flipped through the pages.

Oh, I see! It's a diary.

Oh, wow! She writes a diary!

How cool! I thought.

Well, let me read what she wrote.

Hmmmm... the first one I read was about a guy she was falling in love with.

Oh... I thought. *She's in love.*

I scanned another page. She talked about how she experienced heaven.

What?

Heaven?

She must be so in love that she felt like she's in heaven, I guessed.

I wondered who among the tricycle drivers she was involved with. I flipped the page again and it said,

Dear Diary, mahal na mahal ko si Kuya. Nakarating na naman ako sa langit kagabi. (Dear Diary, I'm so in love with Kuya. I experienced heaven again last night.)

I stopped reading. We needed to leave. We needed to be first in line. I snuck the little blue notebook in my pocket, and we hit the road. Along the way, while the kids were playing in the back seat, I was thinking... well, actually, I didn't know what I was thinking.

What is there to think?

Please help me think what to think.

We checked in, and we waited. I still didn't know what to think, but my throat was dry and my heart was pounding. I needed to hold my chest. I felt my chugging heartbeat in the midst of all the children's noise at the doctor's office. I told my kids to stay with their father, and I went to the bathroom with the diary. I sat down and read the entire thing, from beginning to end. Now, my heart was beating a lot faster. I couldn't breathe. I felt like throwing up.

When she said, "*Kuya* brought me to heaven again last night." I thought it was a different *kuya.* Then somewhere in her diary, she wrote "*Kuya* G***"

Well, Kuya G. is my husband!

Kuya G. is the father of my children!

And Kuya G. is having an affair with our yaya *in our house?*

In our very own house?

When did that happen?

When did it start?

Is that why there were porn tapes in our VHS player THAT time?

Is that why she would always take a shower before midnight?

Is that why she didn't wear an underwear at night?

Oh, God! Please help me.

PLEASE HELP ME!

PLEASE HELP ME!

I felt the **MOST** excruciating pain.

It was unbearable!

I felt like I was in HELL!

I needed some air.

I needed to scream.

I needed to cry.

I needed some water.

There wasn't enough air in that crowded room full of snotty kids running around. I couldn't scream in a room full of children. I couldn't cry. I needed to hold the tears. I still needed to understand what the doctor had to say about Micci. I drank the water from Micci's feeding bottle.

Very calmly, I handed my "FAITHFUL HUSBAND" the notebook and asked, "What is this about?"

Innocently, he replied, "What?"

I hissed, **"This! Read it!"**

He read it while I walked away with my two children. I watched him read. After reading it, I came back to him and said, "So, what is this again?"

With a gentle voice, he answered, "Don't worry about it. It's nothing."

It's nothing?

NOTHING??

SERIOUSLY?

IT'S NOTHING?!

Gritting my teeth, I whispered angrily, "*Fix this! Fix this! I don't want to see this girl again, or I'll kill you both when we get home!*"

Then, Micci was called by the nurse. I tried to pay attention to the doctor. But my brain suddenly stopped working. I even asked Nique to listen to her for me. I didn't hear the doctor, but I saw her smile at me, and I saw her lips were saying something. Thank God, this doctor's appointment is over! At last, we were out of the room.

He brought us to a shopping center near our house while he made a phone call. It took us a while to get home, but when we did, the heaven girl was gone—her room was empty. Now, I was in my own space. I could finally do what I was holding back for hours. I was so mad.

I cried!

I screamed!

Believe it or not, I was very strong that day! I pulled the couch and the bed out of the house all by myself. As the neighbors watched, I told them, "You want a couch? How about a bed?"

"Here!"

"Take it!"

"Take it!"

"Take it!"

"I don't need these things in my house!"

Well, they needed a new couch and a bed, so my neighbor next door took them all. Nique and Micci asked why I gave them away. They asked why I was mad. They wondered why I was crying.

Can I tell them why?

Even if I could, they were not going to understand. I just asked them to hug me, and hug me really tight. That would probably help me stop from crying. And so they did. On each side, I had two sets of tiny arms hugging me.

Did it stop me from crying?

Nope!

I cried even more. I felt so sorry for them. I was stupid. I didn't even see that coming.

Was I too naïve?

Did I trust him too much?

I knew he could be violent, but to go so far as having a sexual affair with the *yaya* in our house?

In our house?

That was insane!

Oh…he makes me vomit!

How did I miss that?

How did I not know they were doing something in my house?

Our house is a holy place!

This is where we raise our children.

How could you disrespect your own house with your family just sleeping in the other room?

You are an animal!

You are a beast!

I thought you were an ex-seminarian?

I thought you knew more than I did?

I thought you understood the church teachings more than I did?

I was so crushed.

My life stopped.

What do I do now?

I prayed. I prayed. And I prayed. I would spend hours in the adoration chapel near my school.

Lord, I don't know how to move on from this.

Did I tell my parents about this?

No.

Did I tell my in-laws about what he did?

Not really.

Did I share it with my friends at work?

No.

But I told everything to Mama Mary.

Yes, she is the one I turn to when I'm lost and helpless. Every day, I was lost and helpless, so I talked to her every day. She is my best friend. She is my Mother. I just sat and looked at her. Then I would cry day in and day out. I was only 27 years old when I felt like I was crucified on the cross. He was my cross, my heavy cross. That voice that talked to me and led me to the room to see that tiny notebook, it was the voice of Mary. She wanted it to stop. She protected me and my children.

I wanted to leave. I couldn't be with this person anymore. I didn't even want to see him. Knowing that he was home freaked me out. Knowing that I was in the same house where he had this thing with the *yaya* made me sick. I didn't want to see this place. I didn't want to wonder what they did in this area, in this room, when they did it, or what I would do if I woke up while they were doing it. God was on my side. He didn't let me see them in action. Mary knows it would be too much for me to see them actually do it.

The horrible thoughts haunted me. I didn't want to walk around the house. I felt stiff. My house felt filthy. I felt dirty just being in this house. I wanted to leave. I wanted to leave with my children, to go somewhere far, some place where I didn't have memories of his infidelity. It was so bad that I couldn't sleep. I felt paralyzed. But I needed to be strong for my children, or at least look strong.

Our narrow driveway was full of non-biodegradable trash. In the Philippines, trash segregation is strictly imposed. So, being the science teacher that he was, he collected all the trash but didn't schedule or figure out a way to dispose them. There were many bags of trash piled at the end of our driveway. I am not kidding, trash bags were stacked up taller than I am. We would always fight about this. It was one of the main points of our usual arguments.

Why couldn't he dispose of the trash after filling up a bag instead of keeping them?

They occupied a lot of space—space that the children could have used to run around and play. Moreover, it was a fire hazard and an eye sore! This made sense to me, but not to him. He thought that since he was a science teacher, he knew better. You don't have to be a science teacher to figure that out; it is common sense, Dum Dum! Whew! I cannot win, so I just let it go. Sometimes, I would hide in the back of our little Daihatsu car and sit there, near the trash. I felt like trash anyway because of how he treated me. I would just cry my heart out.

When will I ever stop crying?

I couldn't stop. It was too hard. My heart was so heavy, full of hatred and disappointment, but also full of love for my growing kids.

What do I do?

I sat there in the corner where no one could see me.

I grieved in solitude.

*****

Life went on, but it was just getting worse. The elements of a good marriage—love, respect, and trust—were not present in our relationship. We didn't love each other anymore; we were just there for the kids. We had no respect, and we didn't care anymore. We had no trust. How could I trust someone who couldn't be trusted in his own home? What a family, right? But I stayed for my children, and I had to deal with the **3 Ps constantly: petty, perennial problems.**

This was our family set-up: do what you want, no one cares. I stayed in the room with my children—no questions asked. He would usually come home late, and I think it's because he goes to clubs to pick up girls (I don't know really but probably.) As long as he drove the car the next day so we could both go to work, we were fine. I wanted to learn how to drive the car so badly, but he wouldn't let me. I could secretly enroll in a driving school, but I didn't have enough money. I watched him drive but never had the courage to get behind the wheel.

Then our old *yaya*, the elderly one, came back. Thank God! I told her everything, and she said one of the reasons why she left was because she knew what they were doing. She couldn't stand it either but didn't know how to deal with it. She also didn't know how I would react if she told me. She was so sorry for me and the children. Thankfully, she was back, and I had someone to talk to. It felt great. Unfortunately, she needed to leave for good because her husband got very ill. I was sad, but I understood. I appreciate her loyalty to me. But thankfully, we found two new *yayas*. They were young, a lot younger than the *heaven girl*. These two were not *heaven*-type of girls, anyway. In fact, they didn't like my husband at all. They thought he was weird, but they stayed because they needed to make some money.

One evening when we were having dinner, we had a fight... again. As usual, it's one of those many fights, and I don't remember why we fought. He was so mad at me. We were seated around the glass dining table that I bought with my 13th month pay (yes, I was in a third world country, but we received bonuses and 13th month pay before Christmas.) I loved that glass table. Anyway, because he was so angry, he got up and hit me so hard at the back of my head. Whoa! My face landed on my plate! Thankfully, my neck was still attached to my head, so I pulled it back up. There was food all over my face. I got up and cleaned up while he was still talking bad at me. I cleaned my face as I listened to his non-stop whining over something.

I questioned myself at that point.

Why is he doing this to me?

Do I deserve this?

Does he really need to do that in front of the new yayas?

Do the kids really need to see that?

Am I a bad mother?

I think I'm a good mother to my children.

But why does he not value what I do?

Perhaps I was a bad wife. I thought maybe it was because I didn't do what he wanted. I refused to sleep with him anymore because I didn't want to be pregnant again. I couldn't have another child because he was very lazy. He was not a good parent at all.

No!

Not anymore.

This has to stop.

I need to fight because this is way too much!

I am not taking this crap anymore!

I grabbed a mug and threw it at him. He ducked. I missed. He picked the mug up and threw it back to me. The yelling and screaming continued. Nique, who was about six years old that time, got off his chair and hid under the table. I cannot forget the look on his face. He sat beside the *yaya's* leg while his eyes followed the mug go back and forth through the glass table.

I was ready to fight.

He wants a fight?

Alright!

I ordered the *yayas* to keep the kids in the room and lock the door. I hit him. He grabbed me. I punched him. He kicked me down, down on the floor. I wrestled. I kicked. I punched. I smacked. I tried every move, but he was a black belt Karate champ, and he knew where to hit me to shut me up. He held my neck and pressed my throat. Still, I tried to kick his balls. *Yeah! Hit him in his balls*! But I couldn't, he was too strong for me. He ripped my clothes off and pressed me harder, much harder on the floor. I fought my hardest. I gave out my best, but it wasn't good enough. He was like a devil on top of me. I couldn't fight any longer. I stopped fighting. I just cried. Tears flooded the floor. I gave up. He warned me not to fight back next time as he grabbed my throat. Then he got off me.

I got up and picked up my torn dress from the floor. That green duster dress was my favorite. I looked for some dirty clothes from the laundry basket and got dressed. I went in the room where my children and the *yayas* were hiding and listening to all that noise. The *yayas* looked at me, but couldn't say anything because they were in shock, too. I got the kids and told them to go to sleep and forget about what happened.

Life must go on.

Then I put the kids to bed.

That was quite a wrestling match.

What does it look like to live in a low-cost housing in a third world country in a province?

Imagine a row of tiny houses maybe around two meters apart from each other. We heard each other's noise especially because the windows were always open to keep the house cool. So our neighbors certainly knew what happened. Our neighbors' dogs were shaken up because I heard them barking. They felt the commotion and tension in that tiny house.

What do I do?

What could I do?

On days when I needed a place to think, I would I sit in my hiding place, the corner where no one can see me. I grieved and cried in solitude. I remember that one hot summer day vividly; I could hear Nique and Micci playing inside the house. They were laughing and just being kids. What did they know? How could I keep them happy?

Lord, help me figure out what is best for my family.

Quietly, I heard little steps coming from behind. It was them, my "little people."

Nique, in his tiny voice asked, "*Bakit ka nandito, Mama? Umiiyak ka, Mama?*" (Why are you here, Mama? Are you crying?)

Then, Micci wiped my tears away with her tiny hands, but more tears rolled down my cheeks.

I love my children so much, and I just want to protect them.

But how? I really didn't know what to do. Can someone help me?

*****

La Salle School is one of the most prestigious schools in the Philippines. It offers great benefits to all the employees. The teachers before me enjoyed the benefit of free schooling for all their children from kindergarten to college. Yes! Great, right? Unfortunately, when I was there, that benefit was no longer available. I know... it was a little sad (but they offered free graduate studies to all its employees.) So Nique, unlike the children of my co-workers, went to Mother of Perpetual Help School instead. It was a school near our house and was run by nuns.

One morning, I got a phone call from the school principal. She said a teacher had found Nique sitting on a plant box, crying, and was refusing to enter the classroom.

That's not my child. He loves school. He is an obedient kid. He follows whatever the teachers tell him.

They called on the principal to handle the issue. According to the principal, Nique was crying because he saw his father beat me up. He saw our fight and heard us yelling at each other, and as a result, he couldn't focus in class. He was very young and was burdened by our messed-up relationship. Poor kid. He wanted to help me and save me, but he couldn't do anything. He was just crying.

Immediately after I hung up, I told the father about what happened in school. This was so heartbreaking. It is interesting how you remember all the details about the things that matter to you the most. I even remember the clothes I was wearing that day. It was a sleeveless printed brown top and a pair of brown slacks.

No, this is my fault.

I fought back, and I made him angry.

I will fix this, it will get better.

In the car, we were blaming each other. Pointing fingers. Your fault. My fault. It had to stop.

I think I am a strong woman. He can beat me up, punch me, cheat on me, and disrespect me. He doesn't even have to love me or take care of me. I can handle all that. I cry. I sleep. I pray. I move on. I can pretend nothing happened, but if it's about my children, if someone hurts them, if they get involved, trust me, I will growl at you. I will do anything and everything for them. They're my life!

We arrived at the school. I saw Nique still sitting on the plant box in his uniform—a bright white shirt and blue shorts. That chunky boy of mine was emotionally affected.

I told him, "It's alright, Kuya Nique. I'm fine. We get along. Here, see? We're together."

Then I hugged him tight, very tight.

Oh, Nique, you have no idea what this means to me.

We walked him around and went to the playground. He got on the swing, and he smiled. He stood in the middle and held our hands. Everything seemed perfect.

"Are you ok now?" I asked.

"Yes, Mama," he replied.

"You think you can go back to your class?"

"Yes, Mama."

"Ok now. Give me a kiss. I love you. I love you very much!"

With another flying kiss and a goodbye, he left.

That was an eye-opener. We agreed to work it out to be better parents. We still argued but more discreetly now. Every day, we still fought. We really didn't get along. For real! Oh well, I would do anything for my children. One more fact about him: he has wild crazy sex thoughts. He was a sex maniac!

Do you know why we argued all the time?

It was because he talked about sex all the time! When we were in the car, all he talked about was sex, sex, and sex! I hated it! I didn't want to listen to him. If I could only jump out of the car, I would. If I could only get a ride from someone else, I would.

Why did we fight?

He forced me to do his sexual acts.

Do you know how painful it is to do things against your will?

Is this what being married meant?

Am I a sexual object?

He only used me for pleasure. I felt like a prostitute on some nights. Sometimes, he would rape me. He would force me to do things I didn't want to do. If I fought back, I would get hurt. If I fought back, the kids would know. They will be broken. I was broken, but it's alright. I told you, I was a tough chick. They say sex is good, but it wasn't for me. It was a nightmare! It was painful! I avoided it. I would make every excuse and find any reason not to have it. I hated it, but he loved it! One time, I said to his face, "You treat me like an object. You keep me in the drawer when you finish using me and take me out only when you need me."

With that said, now I needed to be more patient and not talk back even if I wanted to. I just needed to sacrifice more for my children. We argued again about something, and I was tempted to fight back because he wasn't making any sense (as always). At one point, I got so sick of it that I opened the door on my side and jumped out of the car when we slowed down at the toll gate. If I stayed in the car for another minute, I would just kill him—kill him in front of my young children. I knew it was bad, so I needed to get away. I got out of the car, got on the passenger *jeepney* right behind us and didn't look back because if I looked back and saw my children's faces, I would melt and go back to the car. I needed a time-out from this person. I went to a place where I felt safe and free. I sat in a hospital lobby that night, where I could be away before evil took me. I prayed in the little hospital chapel and went home the next morning as if nothing happened. As a welcome, he accused me of cheating and meeting up with some guy. I took a deep breath and survived the day. Thank God!

In 1998, a big blow hit him hard. He was a P.E. teacher, teaching gymnastics. One high school student complained about him. The student and her wealthy family came to school with a prominent lawyer, accusing him of inappropriate touching. The school principal had a meeting with him, but he denied everything. He was charged of acts of lasciviousness. They asked me to make a statement in his favor, but I couldn't do that without lying. I myself couldn't trust him. In my head and in my heart, I think he did something, but I didn't want to be involved in it. He was crushed. I was crushed for him, but I was just being truthful. To avoid any scandal, he was asked to resign, which he did. It was embarrassing. I was embarrassed, but I needed to stand by my man, so I also had to resign when he did. He transferred to PAREF Southridge (an exclusive school for boys), and I moved to Montessori De Manila. Since those two schools were situated in the same village, we thought it was a good idea. I brought Nique along with me because my new school offered free education to their employees' children. It was a great plan.

This was how our day looked like: I cook at night for the next day. The next morning, I pack our lunch, leave the house, and Nique and I would get dropped off at my school. Then he goes to his school while Micci stays at home with the *yaya*. Then, he picks us up after school, and we go home. When we arrive, I unpack, we eat dinner, and I wash the dishes while Nique does his homework. At the same time, Micci works on her ABCs, numbers, colors, and handwriting. I get up from time to time to take care of some stuff. The *yayas* prepare whatever it is I need to cook while I give the kids a bath, brush their teeth, and comb their hair.

Then guess what? I got pregnant again for the third time!

I wanted to die.

What?

Again?

Oh, God... what will I do?

I can't take it anymore.

Bad things went in my head.

Should I abort the baby?

Is there something that I can drink to lose the baby?

I went to Quiapo and saw all those herbs that people say are good for abortion.

No, I can't do that.

I went to church instead. I prayed. I prayed. And I prayed.

Lord, what will I do? I don't want this anymore. I was already struggling with two kids, and I got another one? He is not a good man. He is so irresponsible. I can't do this alone. I wish I could lose the baby naturally, so I wouldn't feel guilty. Can I wish for a miscarriage?

I jumped 10 times, hoping that maybe I would bleed. I wished I would bleed like when I was pregnant with Baby #2. I wished... I wished ...and I wished... Then, I stopped wishing after 24 hours.

Evil was working. I needed to fight the devil. This baby had nothing to do with all the mess that I had gotten myself into. I went back to church. I was sorry for entertaining evil thoughts. I held my belly and offered my situation to God.

Lord, please take over. Maybe, this baby will help him realize the things that he needs to realize. Maybe he will mature once he has three kids.

I kept the baby. I said sorry to my unborn baby. I stayed healthy and tried to be happy for 9 months. My in-laws talked to me about taking contraceptive pills or considering ligation after this baby. It was a difficult topic. I tried taking pills after Nique, but I didn't feel good about it; it just didn't feel right. To put life-stopping drugs on my tongue every day and put the Body of Christ on Sundays? It's not Catholic. On the other hand, now I was an Asian lady with a big belly!

What is worse?

Feeling guilty or continuing to get pregnant?

My belly got bigger.

"It's ok," I thought. *This will be the last one.*

That year was a real struggle. I was adjusting to my new school with a growing belly while I tagged Nique along as a first grader. What a life, right? I was 29 years old, and my body was so tired. After school, I wanted to throw myself in bed and sleep for days. This was wishful thinking—of course, it didn't happen. Well, the father-driver always picked us up late. I was just glad I had that chunky boy, Nique, to entertain me. But being the overweight kid that he was, he was always hungry. He would finish all the leftovers in our lunch bags and eat even my food.

Do you know what it's like to be pregnant?

You're always hungry.

I was a pregnant lady with barely anything to eat. A pregnant lady who sat outside the school building while everyone else was home already. In the dark, outside, with a tired and hungry first grader and a belly so big, we waited for our *BEST father-driver*. My *patience* was running out.

We had been sitting and waiting outside since 5 p.m., and it was already 8:30 p.m.! Please don't forget I'm pregnant! And this boy is HUNGRY!

We walked to the nearest bakery store where there was light and bought something to nibble on. Then I called from my cellphone. Do you remember those big heavy cellphones in the 90s? There was no text messaging yet, so I'd call:

WHERE ARE YOU?

DO YOU KNOW WHAT TIME IT IS?

DO YOU REMEMBER THAT YOU HAVE A SON AND A PREGNANT WIFE WAITING FOR YOU?

I was mad. Really, really, mad.

Little Child #3 in my belly was hungry.

It's ok baby. I'm sorry, we don't have food, but I'll go find some Spanish bread and drink water.

A Spanish bread would cost 1 peso (about a penny worth).

Then, that familiar car arrived, driven by a man without a soul!

I questioned him, "Where were you again?"

At school, working on your grades? Working on your grades in an air-conditioned room while we sit out here in the dark, and it's hot!

Alright.

Again, I tried my best to control my anger because Nique was watching, and I didn't want to be upset for my unborn baby. I just wanted to be home and hug Micci, who had been waiting.

Fake it, girl.

You have to do it for your children.

Alright.

Lord, please help me.

Then, it was time for Child #3 to pop out of my big belly. I felt the contractions. My bags were packed weeks ago because I knew it would come any time. Who knows! We were an hour away from the city when it happened. We left, but we needed to drop by his school first.

Why?

Because he needed to get the check.

"The check? Why now? That should have been taken care of!" I told him.

All he said was, "I was busy and didn't get the chance."

He went in his school building while I waited on the bench outside. I was hurting, bleeding, and sitting uncomfortably on a stone bench. It took him hours! That meant hours of hard labor for me. I was glad my water didn't break. I sat there and prayed.

Was there anything else I could do?

Did getting mad help?

Nope, it would just make things worse, so I didn't. Finally, he came with a signed check. That was a loan to cover my hospital bills. We were going to a cheaper hospital because I didn't want to contact my former OB-GYN. I'm sure she wouldn't have minded, but she had given me two free deliveries already, and I thought that was enough. Three would be too much. Also, I didn't want her to know I was pregnant again. Luckily, I worked with someone who knew a doctor who delivered babies for free! As one of my favorite songs by Don Moen says, "God will make a way, when there seems to be no way." You know this song?

My new OB-GYN was a nun, can you believe that? A nun-doctor at Our Lady of Lourdes Hospital in Manila. So there I went, with no doctor's fee and a minimum fee for my low-cost room. For Nique and Micci, I stayed in a private room with a TV. Yep! That was a comfortable life after delivery.

With Child #3, it was a loud, crowded, and tight room. I was in the ward, but blessed with a healthy baby girl, who survived long hours of waiting at school and not having the right food at the right time. **Audrie Cuthbert** is Child #3. She had a pointed nose in her tiny pretty face. She is my Chinese doll. I named her **Au**drie because she was the little me, very patient and prayerful. I knew she would be prayerful when she grows up because I spent most of my time praying when she was in my belly. I wanted to see a part of my name (**Au**rora) in hers. What about "Cuthbert," you ask? She was born on March 20, the Feast Day of St. **Cuthbert.**

My third heart, Audrie, was about 5 months old here.

Now, the baby is out. I left Montessori De Manila after a year. I transferred to PAREF Woodrose, an exclusive school for girls. It is a much better school with better teacher benefits. It is the sister school of PAREF Southridge, which was an exclusive school for boys. I was also one semester away from completing my master's degree. Well, I guess my first post-graduate degree is Master of Arts: Major in Child Birth! Haha! I had mastered delivering babies because I had successfully delivered three healthy babies in a span of seven years!

Oh boy!

What did I do with my life?

I lived to poop babies! With three beautiful children and a busy life as a teacher, mother, student, and a *wife* on some nights, I survived the daily fights and yelling (except on Saturdays when I was out for class.)

Is this going end or not?

I thought he would mature and get better. No. In fact, he got worse. My marriage was just falling apart.

Did I fail?

Was this marriage even right in the first place?

I would do anything and everything to make it right for my children.

But when is he going to love and respect me?

These were the questions that lingered in my mind.

Then I thought of a plan. Maybe, if he felt jealous and threatened, he would see my worth. Last time I checked, I was and still am the mother of his children. Shouldn't we be working together as a team for these little angels? So I started taking care of myself a little. I put more shampoo on my hair when I took a bath, fixed my hair a little, and put on better clothes when I went to school. On days when he wasn't really crazy, and we could actually have a peaceful conversation, I would mention in passing that someone in my class always sat next to me. Then, he'd ask questions, which I answered.

I told him, "Well, we are in a group, and we just all eat together and study together while on break."

This triggered him to interrogate me more. He would ask, "What does he look like?"

"Oh, he's alright, but he's tall."

Now, he's furious. At that moment, I felt important. It was working, I guess. He's very insecure about his height, so when I said *"tall,"* I felt the tension. The following weekend witnessed another fight. He wouldn't let me leave with a better-looking outfit. He wanted me to look ugly when I went to school.

I responded, *"Are you serious?"*

In my head I thought, *so this is how you react to this situation? How about starting to think about the kind of husband that you are to me? How about figuring out how to become a good role model to your children? Now, you filter my clothing? Oh no! You can't stop me from going to school. I will finish my degree!*

He got mad, and I got mad, too! He's evil, but I can be evil as well. I made it my mission to make him more jealous! One night, I came home late on purpose. After school, my classmates asked if I wanted to hang out and go shopping.

Did I have money to hang out and shop?

No, but I had some to spend on a movie. I didn't feel like going home anyway. I didn't want to see him. I went to see *A Walk in the Clouds* by Keanu Revees, and I watched it twice, **ALONE! Yes, just me, myself, and I.** Remember, there were no text messages during that time. But even if there was, I didn't have a phone. So I sat there and fell in love with my Keanu. Even though I didn't eat anything because I didn't have money to spend on food, I still had *the best time*. It was freedom! I knew what I had gotten myself into; I was ready for this. And if he kills me, I think I'd be alright. At least I was happy to see my onscreen crush. Haha!

When I arrived home, he flipped! He accused me of cheating. He said I was a whore. He said I was flirting with my classmate. He said bad words about me.

It was ok. But this fight was not over yet.

The next Saturday, I bought a card from our university bookstore, and wrote a cute little note **TO** me and **FROM** me. That's right! A note for myself, written with words I wished he would say to me (I wonder where that card is now. It would be nice to show you what I wrote in it.) I changed my handwriting and mailed it to our house with no return address. Well, duh! It's anonymous. It feels funny now that I'm writing about it. I have never shared this with anyone, but that was one of the craziest things I did when I was younger.

Weird, right? Yes, and it made things worse between us. We fought even more. Now, he was more jealous. Yay! Mission accomplished! But not really because he didn't seem to realize my worth as his wife. He cursed me even more. Despite this mess, I survived all the drama in my life, and I successfully finished my master's degree at De La Salle University with Distinction in October 1999. Congratulations to me! I got a silver medal. Audrie was just eight months old then. God had His ways of rewarding me and keeping me motivated. I thank Him every day.

The day I earned my Master's Degree in Teaching at De la Salle University.

He didn't change in the way I expected. Like I said, my plan didn't work after all, and I got beaten up even more. One time, we were on our way to my in-laws' house as their family from Canada came home for a short vacation. We were going to meet his cousin for the first time. Our little Daihatsu van was loaded with two *yayas*, three kids, the father-driver, and myself. We were fighting before we even pulled out of the driveway. Imagine a two-hour drive of non-stop arguing with a quiet audience in the back of the car. I just couldn't help but talk back at him.

"What do you want? What is wrong with you? Can we just act like we get along because the kids are watching us?"

Nope. That didn't happen. I was in the passenger's seat when he threw a punch at me as we drove on the highway. Driving and punching in the highway? Skillful, huh? Yeah. His strong punch landed on my chipmunk cheek. Karate guy, eh! I saw stars on a bright sunny day, and oh, how they twinkled! My face got stuck for a moment to the car window after he landed the punch. I got a locked jaw. I opened my mouth, stretched my jaws, tilted my head from side to side, fixed it, and took a deep breath. This wasn't going anywhere. I cannot win this. I just kept quiet.

Should we turn around and go home instead?

No. They're expecting us.

Should I just get off the car and let them go?

No. It will make my family look bad. I didn't want them to think that we are not ok. But I was hurting, and I didn't feel like going anymore. I couldn't put a smile on my face. I think I needed a moment by myself. I wished I could be alone, but my kids would miss the fun if we didn't go. Eventually, we arrived and got off the car. I told the *yayas* not to say anything about what had just happened. With warm hugs and greetings, we survived the party. Everybody seemed ok. But I wasn't.

This person never failed to make me feel worthless. I never felt important in our 12 years of being together! Our marriage was like hell. This relationship was just so bad, but again, I needed to pretend like everything was ok. I still didn't tell my parents or his family about our status. Don't get me wrong here. I love his family. Another reason (other than my children) why I kept this marriage for so long was because of them. They treated me right. They valued my worth as a person and mother to their (soon-to-be) four grandchildren. They helped and supported me, unlike him. It was a roller-coaster ride.

*****

We fought, but we never missed going to church on Sundays as a family. I think this is why people think we have a strong family, because we were always together no matter what. However, every time we were at church, I would hear my heart scream and ask for help. I couldn't stand his presence beside me. Just knowing that he was there burned me. I was glad Audrie was just starting to walk. She would wiggle from my arms and point at the floor, indicating that she wanted to walk around. God is really good. He always saves me. For some reason, Audrie would always do that when it was close to "Peace be with you" time. For the non-Catholics, there's a part in the mass where we turn around and shake hands with the people around us and say, "Peace be with you." If you're a family, it's normal to kiss your kids and spouse.

BUT I DIDN'T WANT TO KISS MY SPOUSE!

I DIDN'T FEEL LIKE SAYING PEACE BECAUSE I WANTED WAR!

I couldn't be a liar in the House of the Lord. So, Audrie, my little Audrie, wanted to move her legs. Nique and Micci stayed with their father while I kept Audrie. I would excuse myself and bring her outside to not bother the people inside the church. I would listen to the priest from the outside and be back by the time he said, "The mass has ended. Go in peace to love and serve the Lord." Smart move, right? Well, I needed to be creative. I respect the House of my Lord, but it's just too hard for me to respect the person who disrespected me every day. I thank God for Audrie.

Child #3, like the two older kids, started walking on their own before they turned one year old. I saved up some money for Audrie's first birthday party. We rented a small room at McDonald's and invited some kids. While they were playing and having fun, I was worried. Worried not because there might not be enough food for the kids, but because I hadn't had my period, and I was expecting it that day.

Oh well, the day is not over yet.

Maybe, I'll have it at midnight, or it's just a day delayed.

Well, I was wrong. It turned out ***I WAS PREGNANT AGAIN!***

WHAT?

WHEN AND HOW DID THAT HAPPEN?

Oh, God, You didn't send your Holy Spirit like You did to Mama Mary, did You? But why is this happening?

I was so confused!

Was I sleeping when it happened?

I had no idea. Up until now as I write this story, I still can't remember how in the world I got pregnant with Child #4.

Did he sneak in the room while I was sleeping?

At one point, I confronted God.

I asked him, "Do you love me, Lord? Do you not know what kind of life I live right now? Do you really know who I am? Do you not know what I have gone through? Do you think I am a Superwoman, because I'm telling you, I'm not! I can't do this anymore! I can't have another one."

I wanted to pass out. Then, I was sorry for feeling this way. Again, I prayed for strength for my body and mind.

What will people think of me?

What will my parents and in-laws say?

"Pregnant again?"

Yes, that's what it is.

My belly grew. It grew and grew, and our financial problems grew with it. We barely had anything to eat. My salary was primarily set for the *yayas'* pay and gas allowance. I did more tutoring after work, which meant we would arrive home very late. While I was tutoring, he would park the car at the mall. The kids would do their homework and eat dinner in the car. They also took a nap. My family waited for me, and then we would go home together. As soon as we walked through the door, I would give them a bath, brush their teeth, and tuck them to bed. I could hardly buy my prenatal vitamins.

Also, the food that I ate was not very nutritious, but I prayed a lot harder this time to compensate. I just wanted a healthy baby. Then our Daihatsu van started acting crazy. Our father-driver had only one job, and that was to keep our car running. Unfortunately, being the irresponsible man that he was, he neglected to check the engine regularly. He would miss the oil change schedule for months!

Did I know anything about cars?

I couldn't even move a car.

There were times when our car just broke down in the middle of the highway. Nique, being the chunky kid that he was, would help me push the car to the side while he maneuvered the wheel. The little girls in the car were our cheerleaders and the lookouts. They said encouraging words when I was about to give up. With tiny voices and little heads looking through the window, they chanted, *"Keep going! Push harder, Mama! Push harder, Kuya!"*

What an adventure, eh?

Luckily, we organized a carpool with our neighbor who taught at my school. So when our car was dead, theirs was alive. Likewise, when their car was dead, our car was alive to give them a ride! God always works in mysterious ways! I was faced with financial, emotional, physical, and all other sorts of difficulties when I was pregnant with Child #4. This baby is a survivor! Well, she was born in our worst situation. I was at my lowest. I had four children at 31 years old. I got married at 23 and "manufactured" four children in eight years!

God said, "Go forth and multiply." Well, I guess I took it very seriously and did just that!

We did try to find ways to make more money and to make things work for the children at one point, but for some reason we were not successful. We tried to augment our income by selling fruits like grapes, pears, and apples to our co-workers during the Christmas Season. We went to the store after work and bought them in bulk. I repacked them and sold them at a discounted price. We offered payment plans as well. We also started a small food business, but we were just not lucky. It wasn't for us. We closed out within a year and lost a lot of money. Since life beat us so hard, there was more tension, more fighting, and more pointing fingers as to whose fault it was. It was just non-stop fighting.

The good thing, though, was we enjoyed the free schooling of our three children in our new PAREF School. Nique went to school as a second grader with his father while I had Micci and Audrie, in senior kindergarten and junior kindergarten respectively. It was funny how I never bought school uniforms for them because they were so expensive. Remember, these are exclusive schools. All supplies, uniforms and everything needed to be purchased from the school. But guess what? I never spent money on their school uniforms. The father would check the Lost and Found Box where, thankfully, there were always unclaimed high school uniforms. He would ask permission to get some of those unclaimed items to bring home. I did the same thing in my school. I would ask if I could get a few sets of uniforms before they put them away. Since *Mamang* was a dressmaker, I would send the uniforms with the kids' measurements to my mother in the province. She would make the necessary adjustments and come up with five uniforms for each of the three kids. This means I didn't need to worry about doing the laundry in the middle of the week! Genius, eh?

Meanwhile, Child #4, stayed with our *yaya* at home. Since money was tight, this poor little baby did not enjoy the better kind of formula milk like her older siblings had. The three older ones had *Promil* milk while she only had *Bonamil*, the cheaper brand. Every day, she would eat eggs for each meal. Well, at least the eggs looked different for each meal (give me credit for a little creativity.) Breakfast was scrambled, lunch was sunny-side-up, and dinner would be hard-boiled egg. I know too much egg in one's diet is bad, but it was better than the *bagoong* that I grew up with. I wished I had extra money to buy her some nutritious food, but I was really out of funds. She never had cake on her birthday because I couldn't even afford to buy her milk. It was so depressing to know that I was not providing what should have been provided for my young children. It was not easy, but hey, this kid was a happy baby! She was a happy baby but boy, was she an ugly baby! I wonder what happened to her.

Did it have to do with me not eating good food when I had her?

Or was it because I was so stressed out that she absorbed all my bad emotions when she was still in my tummy?

Every day, when I looked at her face, I felt so sorry.

Why did I have an ugly baby?

Her face was big, her nose was flat with big nostrils, her forehead was wide, and she had slit eyes. But by now, you should already know how prayerful I was. I prayed for God to help me make this kiddo a pretty baby. I massaged her nose and pulled it out while I counted from 1-100. I opened up her eyes and again counted 1-100. I did this all the time. I also cut her eyelashes because old folks said they would grow back long and curly if you trim them while they're still babies. By the way, I did this to the older kids when they were still babies, too. Lo and behold! Before she turned one, I started seeing hope that this kid would grow up to be a pretty lady. When she turned two, she got prettier! And now that she's grown, I watch her with deepest pride when she altar serves or when she gives out communion because God never fails to grant all my wishes. She is perfect! She is one gorgeous looking girl. She is our gymnast and has the most beautiful body of them all. She was asked several times to share her faith with the parents of Edge and Lifeteen Groups (middle school and high school faith formation youth group, respectively) and during Confirmation Retreats. She was also a part of the TLT (teen leaders) group at church and is actively involved in all church activities like her older siblings. Thank God for miracles! I can really say that God makes all things beautiful, and she's one of them. Nothing is impossible with God. By the way, I named Child #4 **Lady Greer** (nick-named Belay) in honor of Mama Mary because I prayed the rosary multiple times while I was in labor at Our **Lady** of Lourdes Hospital in Manila, and because she was born on November 27, the Feast Day of **St. Gregory.**

Check out the transformation: Miracles do happen guys!

*****

Life's challenges always come.

When is this ever going to end?

One day, their father came home and said that the school principal talked to him.

"Talked to you about what?" I asked.

"The school needs to cut down on expenses and lay off some teachers."

He was asked to retire early. Early retirement at age 30? Wow! What a big blow, huh? I wondered who else was asked to retire. Then I started to question him. If he was one of the high-performing teachers in that school, he wouldn't be cut off, right? He must have been at the very bottom of the list in terms of performance. He was not an asset. Also, in that school, all employees, including custodians, have assigned mentees. All students from grades 1-12 report to their assigned mentors on a regular basis. Every semester, the mentors are required to meet with the parents at least once or twice every month (That is unique of PAREF Schools. They believe that parents are the first teachers, and they want them involved.) I had about 19 caseloads from my school every year while he had none. When I asked him why, he simply said he didn't know. In the back of my head, I thought it said a lot about him. So when he said he would be laid off, I wasn't surprised at all. His performance must have been so low that cutting him off was better for the school system. My cross then became much heavier. He was actually my biggest cross!

Really? He couldn't even keep a job?

With four children, how could he be jobless? That meant we needed to pull our belts tighter than ever.

The following year, we had to let go of our *yayas*. I would stay up late at night to cook for the next day. He still drove the car, dropped Nique, Micci, Audrie, and I off at school, then he and Belay hung out in the car all day, parked at the mall where it was shady and windy. Every day, we had this huge green basket where we kept our food for the day. I had the rice cooker on the go, as well. After school, we would eat in the car. I fed the kids before we hit the road, so I just needed to clean them up when we arrived home, help them do their homework, brush their teeth, tuck them to bed, and be ready bright and early the next day. While they slept, I would unpack the green basket, wash all the dishes, and cook for the next day. That was how our weekday looked for the entire year.

At night, when I was all exhausted, I would pause to check on my kiddos. I would watch my four little angels sleep and wonder how to feed them all. I wondered how I could give these children a better life. They didn't deserve this. I needed to do something.

I will not watch my children starve to death.

So I started asking around. I heard about an agency that sent teachers abroad. I knew some of my co-workers from La Salle had moved to California and found a nice paying teaching position. I wanted to try it. I typed up my resume and sent it to two different agencies. I prayed and followed up on it constantly. I made phone calls overseas and spent some of our food money to pay for the calls. I also used up some of our gas money to rent a computer to type up and print out my resume. We didn't have a Wi-Fi or cable, much less a computer or a printer at home. Remember, I lived in a third world country. However, we did have a place called an "internet café" where people could go and do their online stuff. I paid 10 pesos for every hour. That meant I needed to type really fast and get done within an hour or else it would cost me more.

One time, I brought Nique with me to the agency's office to follow up on my application personally. We went there after school. I'm trying to remember where the girls were, but I really can't recall. Maybe they stayed home with their father. It was just me and my chunky boy Nique. It was an hour and a half away from our school. We took the public bus to get there. I knew I had some loose change in my wallet and some bills, so I thought it wouldn't hurt if I went to see what was going on with my application. I just had my heavyweight boy sit on my lap so that I didn't need to pay for his bus fare. He was only in second grade but weighed over 80 pounds! I could feel his weight on my legs, and boy, I thought I wouldn't be able to walk for days! The worst part was, he fell asleep on my chest and drooled on my shirt! To add to that, the smell of his armpits was really strong! I wished I had spare money to get this little bull some deodorant. My legs were hurting, and my chest was tight. He falling asleep on my chest felt like an 80-pound bag of rice was slammed on me. He was so tired after school and baseball practice, he couldn't help but doze off. My tiny, worn-out body remained stiff for over an hour, but I didn't wake him up. Finally, it was time to get off the bus. What a relief! It was like gasping for air after walking in a gas chamber. Thank God for air! We always take it for granted because it's always there, day in and day out. Free for all!

Going back to my after-school agenda, I went to see the agency, and I was told that everything was going well. I just needed to wait and be ready for an interview.

Wow! Alright, chunky boy! That was some good news!

Now, my bus buddy was hungry and thirsty. I checked my pocket and found some coins. I got him Coke and fish balls on a stick. That should hold him for the next two hours. However, I had a new problem: I didn't have enough money for the bus ride home.

What will I do? Should we go to my in laws' house and borrow some money? I can't. I don't have enough money to get there, either. Hmmm...how are we going home?

There was no Uber yet during that time.

I looked in my wallet to see if there was something hidden somewhere. I found nothing except for my broken chain that I had bought when I got my second pay at De La Salle, when I was still single. I had that in my wallet because I wanted it fixed one day. That was precious to me. I always buy something with my pay because I like to see where my money goes. It gives me visuals, and inspires me to work harder. It doesn't have to be expensive. Sometimes, I just buy little things for the kitchen (I love glasses and plates, or any kitchen stuff, by the way.) But when I looked at that chain, I made a decision.

We need to go home.

We walked to the nearest pawnshop, and I pawned my chain for 50 pesos ($1.00). It was more than enough to get us home, but I saved the extra.

One day, I'll be back to redeem my chain. I'll pay the interest and pay them back.

But that day never happened. I never got it back, but at least I got my stinky boy safely back home.

Some days, I would take a day off from work and go to the agency by myself. I spent hours in the line to get lucky. They picked teachers at random to video chat with the hiring officers in California and Nevada. I didn't get lucky this way, but I was told that I had a potential employer in L.A. and Nevada. They were just waiting for some documents. I spoke with the agency director, and I got a good word—a school principal wanted me. I got very excited and resigned from work that school year.

Why?

Because I wanted to spend more time with my children before I left.

Who told me I was definitely leaving?

No one.

Did I have a visa yet?

Nope, but I was going to have it before you knew it. I just wanted to hang out with my little angels before flying.

Guess what?

My wings were broken, and I didn't fly at all. No California or Nevada. Now, this was the worst of the worsts. We were both jobless! Yes, unfortunately. I got too excited and resigned from work without any guarantee that I would be leaving.

That was embarrassing!

My in-laws? I'm sure they wanted to say something but knew it wasn't going to help us. So they just provided for us. His sister, who was a nurse in New York, sent money to my mother-in-law, so she could buy our weekly groceries. When we visited on the weekends, my mother-in-law would cook multiple dishes and give us food for the entire week. Their hearts went for us, especially the kids. There was never a time when they blamed me for my wrong decision. I hated their son at one point, but I have always loved his whole family. They loved me and supported me all the way. They were my family more than my own family in Anda, my province. If there was one reason why I stayed with him after all the fighting and wrestling, it would be his family. I look up to them. I love them more than they will ever know. I did everything I could to save our marriage. I pleaded with God to help me accept this man— to change him, or just change me, or whoever needed to be changed.

I asked God to intervene.

One night, after another big fight, I walked out of the house. It was midnight. I didn't go anywhere far, just around the village. There was no one around but me. I looked up and talked to the stars. They were beautiful! I got too busy taking care of my children and fighting the battles at home. I didn't want to think of anything else; I only wanted to enjoy the beauty in front of me. I remembered the song I sang to my children: "Twinkle, twinkle little star…"

I watched the twinkling stars while walking. Then, I remembered my Pinocchio book with missing pages, the first fiction book I had ever read in high school (yes, in high school… please don't judge me.) The page where Geppetto wished upon the star wasn't ripped, so I knew that part.

What if I wish upon a star?

I looked at the brightest star and wished for someone to really love me. I wondered what it was like to be loved and taken care of. I wondered what it felt like to be important and needed in a good way, not in a lustful way. I wondered and wondered…

Like what I always say, life goes on. I had the chance to talk to one of my La Salle co-workers when I was jobless. She mentioned a particular agency. Since I had an extra copy of my resume, I thought it wouldn't hurt to send it. I put it in an envelope and sealed it with hope and prayer. I turned down my regular tutoring clients. It would have cost me a lot to commute to *Ayala Alabang* (a high-end village where rich people in the south of Manila live) and meet one or two students after school. Tutoring worked for most of the teachers because they got picked up by the driver and dropped off after the session. That was hassle-free and saved us some commute money. Also, I lost my confidence because I resigned and let people know that I was leaving and it didn't follow through. I didn't want people to see me and ask me questions about what happened. I wished I could hide, but I couldn't. I needed to keep my family alive. Luckily, I was recommended by my friend to tutor one girl in our neighborhood. That was good. I didn't need to commute, and I didn't need to spend money on bus fare. I walked every day at 11 a.m. to tutor.

Don't forget your umbrella, Asian lady!

Yes, I used my umbrella on a hot sunny day. While I walked, I prayed the rosary. I talked to Mary and poured my heart out to her. I couldn't help but cry while I walked because I didn't know what else to do.

What will I do, Mama Mary? You are a mother, and you know what is in my heart. I tried everything, but it is just getting worse. The more I try, the harder it gets. Sometimes, I just want to give up. Should I give my children away?

No, I will never do that.

My mother suggested that we move to *Anda* because it was a lot cheaper to live there.

No, I don't want to go back home as a failure. I still have my pride. With my marriage falling apart and life in a total mess, that's the last place on earth that I would go to.

But I needed to be strong for my children. I needed to hold my head up.

We can do this!

We lived one day at a time. In the morning, I left my children at home to earn a living. Nique was eight years old, Micci was five, Audrie was three, and Belay was about two. Big Brother Nique was in charge. I made them food and set it on the table. Each one had a plate. Chunky boy fed them and entertained them until I got home. They could do whatever they wanted, except open the door for someone and play outside (I know I'll get in BIG trouble if I do that here in the US. That would mean some serious jail time for me.) Thankfully, they were obedient children. Nique, always the dependable Kuya, kept them safe. But our house would look like a zoo when I got home. With dirty dishes all over the place, toys everywhere, books, pencils, crayons in all corners, they kept themselves happy and safe.

Where was their father, you ask?

Actually, I don't know. As I write this part, I was thinking where in the world he was during this time. I have no clue. What I do know is when they heard the special knock at the door, they screamed excitedly because I was home. Them happy to see me back home was one special love. As a reward for them, I stopped by the store and bought *jelly ace*, one each. Simple joys for my simple people.

There was one time when we skipped a meal because the mother of the girl I tutored forgot to pay me. After our session, I was hoping that she would hand me the payment, but she did not. I thought it was rude to ask for it, so I went home with a heavy heart. For our next meal, I sent Nique to the retail store across our house with a note asking if we could get a small can of sardines, four eggs, and a kilo of rice. I promised to pay them back as soon as I got paid. Around this point in time, we haven't paid the mortgage for both houses (Remember, he got a house before we got married, and I got one under my name because I had the feeling our marriage would not last, considering he was mean and physical with me.) This was when I felt like I was nailed to the cross. I felt so dead and helpless. **This, I think is the saddest moment in my life,** but I kept believing that even though God gives us bumps in life, He always sends His angels to be with us as we go through our daily struggles. He surrounds us with people who alleviate our pains and sorrows. The girl I tutored and the store owner who loaned us rice and eggs were God's helpers. They provided for our immediate needs.

That one line from the song *Footprints in the Sand* has a strong impact on me. When the man in the song asked God where He was when he needed him the most, God replied, "When you see only one set of footprints in the sand, it was when I carried you."

Very true! I can't help but cry as I write this part because it brings back memories—memories of tears, hardships and sorrows. I don't even remember laughing around this time. I was in my most difficult time. How can I forget the time when I thought God had forgotten me or had taken me for granted? He never left my side. I forgot that He was in the girl whom I tutored, and to *Aling Rosing* (God bless her soul), the owner of that store.

Thank you, Lord, for reminding me that you kept your angels watching over us the whole time.

I'm sorry, Lord. I am not perfect, but You made Your presence known when I was about to lose my faith. Thank You!

Wait, I need to take a break. I need some air. I can't stop crying every time I think about this part of my life. I am a little overwhelmed. I just need a moment, guys.

[A day later...]

Ok, I'm back. I thank God every day for His kindness. I didn't hang out with friends because I didn't have time. Other times I simply chose not to. I couldn't face anyone from work. I didn't want people asking how I was after leaving work. There was no good news at all. I would rather hide and keep things to myself. As I walked to my tutee, I prayed my daily rosary and asked for a sign.

Is there a better life after this? Will there be an end to all these sufferings? When is this going to be over? I am so tired, Lord! Will I ever get a job in the US? Why do other people get a chance, and I don't? Lord, please let me go. I only need one phone call. That's all I need. I will do everything to impress my employer. They will not regret hiring me. I am a good person. I am a good teacher. I will do everything to be of service to whatever school district I will be assigned to. Please give me a sign. Show me one rose flower, Mother Mary. Give me some hope because I am about to give up.

As I walked back home after my session, I saw one big white rose in someone's yard. I couldn't believe I was seeing one! I blinked a couple of times and thought, *Am I hallucinating?*

I knew I was hungry, but I wasn't hallucinating. I closed my umbrella.

Maybe, it's just a shadow or something, because I don't remember seeing that flower this morning! How did I miss it?

I had goose bumps! I wanted to scream.

Is this real?

Yes, it was a real white rose.

But it was white, not red or yellow. Wait... I wasn't specific with the color.

I just asked for a sign, a rose flower, and there it was!

When I got home, my cellphone rang. It was from the agency! They had received my resume sealed with hope and prayer. The lady told me that I needed to report for an interview ASAP.

Wow!

Unbelievable!

The white rose, the phone call, the interview... they were all coming together.

Thank you, Lord! Thank you, Mama Mary!

6
CHAPTER

Got Hired

O ne of the most important days in my life had arrived. I showered and washed my hair. This time, I used the entire Pantene packet of shampoo and conditioner. I put on my professional outfit and got the kids ready to hit the road. While getting their bags and feeding bottles ready, I was thinking of the possible questions that might be thrown at me and how I would answer those questions intelligently. I couldn't afford to fail this interview. Our future depended on the result of that day. I was fired up and ready to grab the job.

"Come on, driver. Wake up! I can't be late. We need to get going!"

We hit the road and dropped the kids off to my in-laws' house. I was running because I was a few minutes behind. I got there, checked in, and sat down. Looking around, I saw a long line of teachers from different top-notch schools.

Oh, God, please help me.

I took out my journal and started writing down my feelings to de-stress.

Then, they called my name.

This is it, Aurora!

Seize the day!

Alright, it's all on you.

I walked in with the brightest smile and greeted the interviewer, "Good morning!"

He replied, "Good Morning! How are you today?"

I got confused.

Did he really want to know how I was feeling that day?

Well, I could tell him how I woke up so early to get ready and how I fixed my children's stuff, dropped them off, got caught in the morning traffic, etc.

But looking back, I'm glad I just smiled because then he started talking. I was on cloud nine as I watched him talk. He was a bearded American guy. I felt like a little kid in front of Santa Claus. I felt so safe beside him that I lost track of what he was saying. All I wanted to do was put my head on his shoulder. I had been so tired all my life, and to lay my head on his broad shoulder for a few minutes would be very comforting.

Alright, Aurora! Wake up! You don't want to blow this chance. Get back on track! Alright?

Alright!

I listened, and we just talked about stuff. I was ready to answer questions about curriculum and educational strategies, but none of those was discussed. We were just laughing. Then he started talking about the Richmond Public Schools District in Virginia and how it could be very challenging in all aspects. He talked about the kind of students and parents that I would be dealing with. He had one question that I couldn't answer, though. He asked what I knew about Virginia.

Hmmm... Virginia? What is Virginia? Is that a book? I have no idea!

Remember, I grew up without a TV or electricity, and I went to a school without a library? And I was out selling *Nutribuns* and learning how to gut fish when I should have been learning about math, science, history, and reading! But I looked professional in my outfit, so I also needed to sound and act professional.

With a smile on my face, I replied, "You know, I haven't really heard about it. Would you like to tell me more about it?"

Classy, eh! Then he started talking about the seasons. He spent more time talking about the fall season. I could tell that was his favorite. He described how leaves changed color.

What?

Really?

Leaves change color?

I didn't know that!

He talked about how Virginia is not as busy as New York but a beautiful place to raise a family. To end the session, he gave me a CD about the Richmond Public Schools District. He wanted me to look into it, learn more about it, and come back that Thursday for orientation (by the way, I still have that CD in my binder.)

What?

I made it?

Am I in?

Yes, I'm definitely in!

I hugged him tight and couldn't thank him enough. I checked out and received the form about the orientation. I walked out of the room, and I sat for a moment.

Is this real?

I don't want to wake up if this is a dream.

I cried and cried and cried. Not tears of sorrow this time, but tears of joy! This was the start of a new life for my family. I didn't go to my in-laws' house to pick up my kids. I didn't tell anybody yet. I walked from the hotel where I had my interview to Don Bosco Church where I got married. Mind you, I had no umbrella this time. I didn't mind the sun kissing my face. I basked in the warmth of God's love. I prayed and thanked God for that monumental event. But I felt something was missing. I needed to talk to someone. I needed to share my joy to an actual person. I looked around and saw other people praying at church.

I realized that's what people do at church—they pray! But I can't just sit next to them and start a conversation, duh? But I was so happy, and I wanted to talk to somebody!

Aha! I know what to do!

I went inside the Confessional Box. I knelt and talked to the priest. I talked about how thankful I was for what had happened to me a few minutes ago. He said he was also happy for me and then blessed me. Then, I was ready to go home. I shared the good news, and everyone rejoiced! I will never forget that overwhelming feeling. Everything seemed ok. No more *yayas,* so no more distractions. I guess the father will just keep his eyes on me and not have any temptations from other girls. The fighting calmed down a little, and we had no choice but to fix our relationship.

After that, there was less tension in our household. We got to sit down and plan the future. We brainstormed what we should do when I leave. We talked about paying off the house, finishing the construction of our dream house, etc. I just asked for one year—one year to get me settled and pay off my loans.

Next came the Orientation Day. The Richmond Public School Executive Director came to interview and hire Special Education teachers. Out of the 75 teachers that he interviewed, only 10 were hired, and out of the 10 he hired, I was the only regular education teacher (with zero Special Education Units).

Answered prayer?

Yes, indeed!

My heart was bursting with joy! Thank You, God! Thank You, Jesus! Thank You, Mama Mary!

As a requirement for us to leave, we needed to register for classes on U.S. Education and Policies. We were also told to practice rolling our tongue a little bit and work on that thick Filipino accent, so I started watching English movies.

Our group met on the weekends at the University of the Philippines (UP) for an all-day class. It was fun; we were like college kids again. We hung out after school, and like my experience in the past, they would eat out while I just watched. I could spend some time with them, I just couldn't buy food for myself. I had an excuse though: "I will eat dinner with my children."

Trust me, I would've loved to hang out, really hang out and enjoy a meal with my group. Sometimes they would stop by Starbucks and grab a drink (Yes, we do have Starbucks in my country, but I had never dared enter or see what was in there.) I knew I couldn't afford it. When I was with them, I only sat and looked around. I paid attention to what they ordered and thought, *"Maybe one day, I can try it when I get the chance."* But guess what? That day never came. I left the Philippines in 2003 and never got to try it. I didn't know what Starbucks coffee in the Philippines tasted like until March 2018, when I came home to visit *Mamang* and my *Ate*. Actually, it took me a while to acquire its taste. Every time my co-worker and I go to Starbucks to chit chat after work, I still think it's overpriced. It's only a *little* better than rice coffee (Just kidding!)

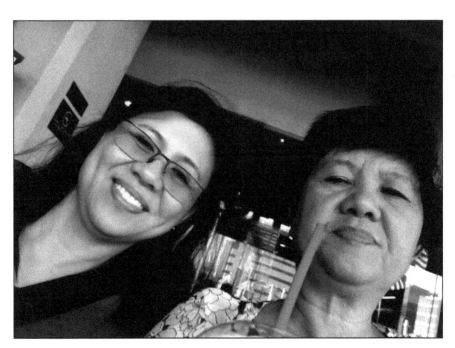

Hanging out with my *Ate* at Starbucks when I came home in March 2018.

My 30-unit U.S. Education class cost 30,000 pesos.

Where did I get that money, you ask?

Well, two of my husband's aunties loaned their money to me. Like what I have said before, I love his family dearly. I can only say great things about each one of them. Towards the end of the course, we were required to go to the University of Baguio (UB) to get our certificate.

I was confused because I was expecting to get it from UP (University of the Philippines), but we were told that we were only using it as a venue. We were actually enrolled in UB and should physically be there for at least a day to authenticate the enrollment. I am not sure if we can do this in the U.S., but apparently, it works in my country.

Anyway, the day that we needed to travel to UB was yet another test on my character. We were on a public bus and were set to travel for hours. It was late at night when the bus stopped for a midnight meal. Once again, I couldn't order anything, and everyone enjoyed their Jollibee meal. I looked again and just ordered the cheapest item there was. They wondered why I was getting a small meal.

I told them, "I am not hungry. I had a big meal before we left."

Big meal? Liar!

I couldn't even remember when I had a real big meal. I always ate left-overs from my children's plate.

Sometimes white lies come in handy to save your face.

My next issue was getting money to pay all the necessary fees which included travel fees, visa fees, transcript validation fees, and airline tickets.

Can I bring my soul to the pawnshop like what I did with my chain? Where will I get all this money?

What's worse was they needed the fees in U.S. dollar, cash! That meant I needed to gather a huge amount of money in pesos and buy dollars from money exchange outlets. I wasn't complaining, I was just wondering where in the world I would get this huge amount of money. Again, his family pulled out all their funds and put them on the table. I needed more, though.

I went to my province and talked to my sister. We did one crazy act without her husband knowing it. We pawned her house title to someone in exchange for 100,000 pesos for a running rate of 3,000 pesos interest rate per month.

That's huge!

But I needed the money, so we completed the transaction. That made my whole body shake.

What if this job is fake after all? What if there was really no job waiting for me in Virginia? What if it is all a money scam?

The thought haunted me. There were a lot of cases at that time where teachers thought they had gotten the job overseas but got dropped off somewhere because they had fake visas. That would be the greatest disaster of my life, and my brother-in-law might kill me! I was putting people's lives at stake.

How will I repay all my debts?

Lots of what-ifs were in my head.

Lord, I asked for a sign, and You did give it to me. I offer all of this to You. May Your will be done!

I finished my class, paid the fees, and waited for my passport and visa. Time to prepare those I will leave behind. I spent some quality time with my children. I talked to them and walked through what was about to happen.

"Mama will be gone, but I will call every day. Make good choices. Make me proud."

We got two new *yayas* to help the father out with the kids. I just needed to trust him again. I gave them a crash course of what to do with the children. I talked to them about homework, food, brushing their hair, cooking, and laundry, the usual stuff. Being the teacher that I am, I came up with a chart to help them remember. My mind said I was ready to leave, but my heart said I was not.

My flight was scheduled on August 14, 2003, the day after my 36th birthday. This was my biggest birthday present. Normally, a birthday to me was just another day on the calendar because I grew up not celebrating it anyway, but that day was *THE BEST DAY!* It was bitter-sweet. Bitter because I knew I would miss my kiddos as I was so used to being around them, but sweet because of the bright future ahead of them.

My promise to my children: "One year, guys! All I need is one full year. I will pay all our debts, and I will secure my job, so I can get all of you."

And my words to the father: "Be responsible! Don't mess this up. We will start all over. We will forget the past and start anew."

I didn't pack a lot of clothes because I could only bring two 50-pound bags and a hand-carry luggage. My children's baby albums were over 50 pounds already. My wooden *Sto. Niño*, a Christmas present from my friend who is also Micci's godmother and a former co-worker from La Salle (Suzette Balgos), and my "little *Sto. Niño*," which was always placed by my bedside when I was in college, were tucked safely in my luggage. Then, it was boarding time. I got chills and goose bumps! The plane took off. This was surreal! I couldn't help but think about my children when the flight attendant served my first meal airborne.

I wonder what they had for dinner. How can I swallow this good food when I can't share it with them? I promise, as soon as I get my first paycheck, you will get the biggest meal at Jollibee! Audrie, drink as much milk as you want. Belay, you can take a break from eating eggs. Eat whatever you want. We'll buy a cake even if it's not anyone's birthday. Micci, order whatever you want. Get the largest French fries—you don't have to share. They will each have their own food. And Nique, get the biggest burger there is! The father, you don't have to work. Just keep an eye on the kids.

I was ecstatic knowing that I could provide for all their needs and wants. Our life was about to turn around!

Being a typical Filipino mother, I saved my airplane food.

And the dishes? I wiped them off and dropped them in my paper bag discreetly. Some folks said I could keep them. Literally, I took everything that I could take. Duh!

We got off at the Houston, TX airport. I claimed my bags and hung my paper bag of "collections" on the luggage handle. Accidentally, however, the bag ripped and there went my food and dishes and stuff from the plane, scattered on the floor!

Ha!

Embarrassing!

Yep!

As gracefully as I could, I knelt down and picked them up one by one while people watched me. Some of them might have been judging me or felt sorry for me. It doesn't matter—didn't bother me anyway. I needed to save everything because I only had $50 as my pocket money. I was going to have to extend my dollars until I got my first pay.

Then, the flight from Houston, TX to Richmond, VA landed.

Wow! I am really in America!

What's up, Virginia?

It's nice to finally meet you.

I heard about you from "Santa Claus."

We were the first batch of hired teachers from the Philippines to join Virginia schools. Three teachers were assigned to teach in Hanover County Schools and seven of us were assigned in Richmond Public Schools (RPS). We, the RPS ladies, shared a three-bedroom apartment at Luton Lane on the Southside of Richmond. There were lots of things to learn—new country, new school, new weather, new culture, and numerous new beginnings and first-times. My first (ever) phone call was to Hawaii. I called my godmother/auntie *Maring* (the pigpen owner) to let her know I was in the USA. We talked for hours! She was so proud of me. Unfortunately, I didn't get to thank her personally because she passed away a few months after I arrived. (May she rest in peace.) Then I used my first phone card to talk to my children and my family in *Anda*, my hometown. By the way, there was no Skype, Facebook Messenger, or video calling yet at that time. I normally spent around $500 every month on phone cards alone. I told their father about my "firsts." First bus ride to go to the city hall to fill out more paperwork, first meeting... lots of firsts. But most especially, my first check. It was a $1,000 relocation allowance to help us settle down. Then I would talk to my children to ask about how their day in school went and what kind of homework they had. We exchanged stories about their teachers and classmates (the good and the not-so-good ones.) We would talk for hours! We laughed and giggled, giggled and laughed, but there was always a pinch in my heart when it was time to say goodbye and hang up. God knows how I missed my children.

Thank you, Dr. Harold Fitrer (the one who interviewed and hired me from the Philippines) and Mrs. Daisy Greene (my first RPS principal) for believing in me! I will be forever grateful for giving me and my family a second chance.

7

CHAPTER

Finally... It's Over!

Everything was set here in Virginia. My teaching job was not fake. Thank you, Lord! It was time to work hard and pay the bills back home. I sent back most of my pay and left a couple of bucks for myself. My mission was to pay off all my loans and be ready to get my family within a year. Remember? This was my promise to my family: "Just give me one full year, and you will all be here with me. We will be together again as one family. We will start a new life. We will put the bad experiences behind us and reset our lives."

I would call home almost every day because I missed my little angels. On weekends, I would wake up early to be the first one to use the landline in our apartment. I was always excited to listen to my children's tiny voices.

I remember sharing my story about my new acquired skills through the phone. I talked about how we had a fancy washing machine and dryer in our apartment. I didn't need to wring the clothes! Talk about upgrade now, huh! Unfortunately, I got too excited and threw all my clothes in the dryer and some of them shrunk, so I ruined some of my thrift store clothes. Also, I told them about how I stayed up late to write my lesson plans on yellow sheets of paper because I didn't have a computer. My lesson plans were supposed to be about Virginia studies, but I was confused because I didn't even know what to teach about Virginia.

What do I know about Virginia?

I had just arrived, and all I knew was the place where I lived, Luton Lane. I also talked about how Americans always said, "How are you?" but didn't actually want to know all about you, unlike back home. I shared my story about my experience of the first frost, my first snow, my class, my carpool to school, what I ate, etc. Then they would tell me their stories about their school, teachers, classmates, and what they ate that day. I asked if they still had milk in the refrigerator, and what their weekend was going to look like. Oh, they are my little joys! They were the reason I was doing all this hard work here in the US. I always looked forward to seeing pictures of Belay, so I could keep track of her looks.

I had all my faith in this baby, that she will be pretty. What was heart-wrenching was when Micci told me that Audrie always slept beside the dress that I wore last so that she could smell my scent. She missed me sleeping beside her. Oh boy, that thought really broke my heart! I wished I could be in all places doing things at the same time. Then I shipped my first package, a huge box, just before Christmas. I bought them gifts that they wanted, and that was so fulfilling!

One thing I did that wasn't safe, though, was to walk to Food Lion by myself on September 8, 2003 (three weeks after I arrived in Virginia). I was going to buy a bouquet of flowers to offer to Mama Mary for her birthday. Apparently, the crime rate in that area was unpredictable, but I still braved my way there. Thankfully, nothing bad happened to me. I took the public bus to downtown Richmond to attend the mass at St. Paul's Catholic Church. I cannot forget how I offered myself humbly to Mary as I looked at her statue. It was she who held my hand and intervened for me. I never missed going to church, and I still buy her flowers every year on her birthday. It's the least I can do. At our church, I stop by her statue before I head to our favorite pew. Belay commented once about how I have a special thing for Mary, and she's right.

On weekdays, I would put all my mind and energy to teaching and adjusting to the new school system. I did everything I could to renew my contract and to fight homesickness. It is very depressing to be away from your family, but I took comfort in the fact that there was a better life in store for them. I missed sleeping with my little angels. I missed cooking for them. I missed giving them a bath, brushing their teeth, and combing their hair. I missed everything that I did with them.

Then one day, Micci said over the phone that she saw her Papa with the new *yaya* on the bed.

What?

In our house—with your children, in the new house?

Not again!

I just left.

Didn't we talk about our plan?

Can you not live a clean life for your children?

Have you forgotten about finishing our dream house?

A few days later, I got a phone call from my sister, who confirmed that he was indeed sleeping with the *yaya... again!*

Didn't I say we would fix our life?

Can you not focus on your four children while I'm gone?

Oh, goodness!

Here I was, trying my hardest to make a living, so I could provide for them while he had only one task: to take care of the children! I had the chance to watch some good movies here in the US, but I'd rather not because I was saving all my pennies and dimes. I bought brand-new clothes and uniforms from the thrift store and Goodwill while some of my roommates went to the Williamsburg outlets to buy designer clothes and accessories. Midschool year, I started applying for a summer teaching job to earn more, so I could buy what they needed when they come over. I also needed to save to purchase their airline tickets. I needed to buy them winter clothes, jackets, blankets, and snow boots. I had to have extra money to buy them ice cream and treats as well.

I worked too hard for my family. That is your family too, jerk!

What else do I need to give up and sacrifice for my family?

I stopped sending him money. Instead, I sent the money to my in-laws, which, of course, made him so mad. He thought it was inconvenient for him to drive for over an hour to get to their place to get money for his bills. But he didn't work when I left, which meant all he had to do was focus on taking care of the kids.

Dude!

Exasperated, I told him, "You're fooling around again! You are hopeless! You are not going to change. No, you don't want to change. FINE!"

Then he would call me names.

FINE!

He said he wanted to go to school and take some classes. He said he needed a computer to do his work. He said it was time to pay for his phone, water, and electric bills. He got all of that.

Just give me my children!

On one occasion, I got a strange text message from him about meeting with me to watch a movie.

It is midnight here in the East Coast, and you want me to see a movie with you?

That was weird.

Oops! Apparently, he accidentally sent me the message that was meant for his girlfriend!

God is good! He always warns me.

This man has lost his mind. He has lost his senses.

I thought we had cleared out our issues when I left. I was so eager to finish the school year because that was when I would know if I would be rehired. I wanted to start processing their papers as soon as possible. I just needed the assurance that I can feed my family when they come. I didn't waste a second when I came here; I worked hard to secure my tenure and be debt-free before I could move on to the next part of my plan, which was to bring them over. But it takes two to tango.

Your wife is in America. There is a great life ahead for you and your family. What happened to fixing your life, and us working things out? Remember, I promised we would start anew? You just had to do what you needed to do as a father, and I would do the best I could to get rehired, so I could bring you all over. I said I just needed one year. Just one! We were going to be reunited and become a happy family, hopefully. Can't we get our life together to save our marriage? At least for the children?

It didn't happen. I connected the dots, which led me to see that he really didn't love me. He wanted something else. It was over. I just wanted my four children.

Every time I called, we would end up cursing at each other. I never cursed until I married this jerk. I would cry after each phone call with him. My blood boiled, and I would always find myself feeling mad. So mad that just hearing his name shook me up. Everything about him just riles me up!

Why was I never happy with this man?

Did he even try to make me feel important?

Maybe he did. In bed. But I was disgusted.

If he did love me, he wouldn't have hurt me. He would have taken care of me. He should have appreciated me. He should have respected me. But I think he just owned me and used me for pleasure. I lost myself and didn't know who I really was. I was my worst self when I was with him.

The war was officially on! We fought every day, exchanging nasty words to each other by phone, email, or text. I would need to exit the apartment when I talked to him on the phone because I became really loud whenever I dealt with him. If my voice could punch, I would swing my arm in my phone speakers. It was that bad! And every time I hung up the phone, I felt like exploding. I have never felt that furious with anyone but him. He brought the worst out of me, and it was not right. I knew I was becoming a bad person. I used to be very prayerful and patient, but God, help me! He sucked out all my good qualities.

Is this what life is all about?

To spend it with the person who infuriates you daily? I don't feel good anymore.

Well, he had been fooling around, so I gave up. I was not going to beg him to love me. It had been 12 long years of cursing, wrestling, yelling, and fighting. Thankfully, my roommates got invited to Filipino parties almost every weekend here in Virginia. The parties gave me a chance to forget about my problems back home for a few hours. I needed to be strong for my children. And consistently, I introduced myself as a married woman with four kids back home. I had no intentions of meeting someone here.

Besides, who in the right mind would want to be involved with someone like me with a loaded package?

No one!

A few weeks after we came in 2003, hurricane Katrina hit Virginia. Schools were closed. We lost power and water in our apartment. Since we got several days off, some of our single roommates went out and met some guys from the other side of the town. One night, they invited them over to our apartment. I was a little upset when they came over. In my head I thought, "*Why do we have male guests in our place? Don't they know it is 9:00 p.m.? It's time to go to bed.*" Besides, I felt invaded and impure. There were three gentlemen—two were younger, and one was 46 years old. They were in the living room, chatting, drinking beer, and just telling jokes. We, the married ladies, were introduced and joined the conversation for a few minutes. It felt weird to be around other men in the house because I was never around a man after I married my children's father. It felt dirty, so I just sat by the steps to keep my distance. From afar, I noticed this funny guy who made us all laugh the whole time. He cracked everyone up with his corny Filipino jokes, and for the first time, I felt my jaws getting tired of laughing. I had forgotten how to laugh because I had been crying for years from dealing with my messed-up married life.

Wow!

It felt good to have a good laugh after all these years! Before they left, he invited all of us to have lunch the following weekend at a Filipino restaurant after church. That was another funny afternoon with everybody.

After that, they came to visit and check on us occasionally. They became our friends. The funny guy would see me handwrite my lesson plans. He said he could find a desktop for me to use if I wanted to.

Of course, I did!

One of my roommates knew how to play *Tong-its* (a card game). He and his friends would come over to play cards with our roommate while I did my usual stuff—lesson planning and studying what to teach the following day.

This guy, the funny guy, became my friend. Nothing special... he was just always available when we needed him.

I didn't know how to drive at the time, so I used to catch a ride with my co-worker every day. For months I carpooled and shared gas money. I would've loved to stay longer at school on most days, to study for my Virginia Studies lessons, gather some visual aids and student worksheets, and get to know the people I worked with, but because I couldn't drive, I needed to pack up when my co-worker had to leave. My school district recognized that we, the Filipino teachers, were dealing with this issue, so they enrolled us in a driving school to help us. We practiced driving at a high school parking lot, and I actually moved the car forward, backward, and around the lot.

That was awesome!

On days when my schedule was open, the funny guy would teach me how to drive. After a few days of practice, I was on the road. Now, I needed to save money to buy a car. I wasn't picky—I just needed a vehicle to get me from point A to B. This funny guy offered me his extra car until I got my own car. He said it was important because I needed to get my life going and not depend on my co-worker for a ride.

Well, who says no to that offer?

One early Saturday morning, he came to pick me up. We stopped by 7-11 to get coffee and a hotdog. Then we went to the DMV to get my license, and the next thing I knew, I was on my own, driving behind the wheel! To make sure I could get to my school safely, he showed me how to use the side roads to alleviate the stress. This way, I could just drive slowly and gain confidence with driving before hitting the highway. He just wanted to give me the mobility to get to places and be at my workplace without depending on anybody. He gave me the confidence and independence to be on my own. He gave me his Honda car.

Sometimes, he would call and ask if there was anything we needed. For the first time, I felt loved and protected. It felt good to be checked on. I remember the first time he and I talked alone. I felt safe and energized. I was very happy. I remember just laughing and exchanging jokes. I was with the father of my four children for 12 years, but I had never felt this way before. It took me only 10 magical minutes to realize that I had spent years of my life crying when I should have been laughing. Those were the happiest and life-changing 10 minutes of my life.

He never asked me out. He respected that I was married and just wanted to help. I enjoyed every minute that I talked to him. Looking back, I realized that my children's father and I never sat on a bench together, watched TV together, or laughed together. We had been married long enough, but I never felt important. Now, here comes this guy, the funny guy whom I just met. He made me feel valuable without expecting anything in return. I am not going to lie... I was falling for this funny guy. His name is Mario. He is my super hero. He is my Bossing. I knew it was wrong, but it felt right for me.

Yes, it wasn't right to have feelings with someone while I was still married.

Yes, I knew and will not forget that I have children.

Yes, I was aware that I am a teacher, and I should be a role model to my children and students.

Yes, I knew that it was immoral and against God's commandment.

Yes, I knew that I committed adultery.

Yes, I knew that I was not worthy of God's grace because I am not clean.

Yes, we both had feelings for each other.

Yes, we had chemistry, and we couldn't fake it.

Yes, we knew that our blossoming relationship was wrong.

Yes, we knew that we were Richmond's Breaking News to the Filipino community because he was the most eligible bachelor at that time.

Yes, we knew that nobody approved it, even his mom.

Yes, we both looked dirty.

It was against all odds.

But I knew there was someone who understood me and knew what was truly in my heart: my Mother Mary. I told her how happy I was every time I was with Bossing. I asked for forgiveness from God, but I promised I would fix the situation. All the degrading comments, gossips, and gnarly looks from the Filipinos who saw me at the stores or at church were sometimes unbearable. But I guess that was a normal reaction. I am not a statue; I heard them, I saw them, I felt them, but I didn't let them and their opinions control my life. It is a lie to say that the daily gossip that most people feasted on about our relationship didn't bother me, because it did. But I chose not to care. I had sacrificed more than enough for my family, and to save a little space for my personal happiness was all I wanted. I learned to love myself, and I deserved to be happy. I am sorry, I am not perfect. I am a sinner, but I never failed to hear mass. I knew my Sunday obligation. However, because of the guilt, I did refrain from receiving the Holy Communion.

I was ready to be judged by all. I will only live once, and I didn't want this chance to slip out of my hands. I just didn't want to be sad and miserable for the rest of my life. Don't you think I deserved a second chance?

Mario was accused of being a home wrecker, but my home was already wrecked by the person I was married to. It was wrong, but I promised I would make this right. It was my decision to be with him. I called and talked to my children's father and told him that I found someone who respected me. It was over. Again, we fought.

What else is new?

He said he would kill all our children. I called my mother-in-law to make sure the kids were safe. It was messy! There was just so much said that cannot be unsaid.

After teaching summer school immediately after my first year in Virginia, I went to see my cousin Anabel and her family in New Jersey in August of 2004. Her husband, Gary was a retired captain at Jersey Police. He and I had a very long conversation about life. That was the first time I really opened my heart to someone, and I only met him a couple of hours after he and my cousin picked me up at the airport. It was an enlightening conversation. God spoke His words through him. I learned that there were things that I could have done to prevent myself from having to endure the things I did while being married to this jerk!

The most important lesson I heard from him was that I could actually call 911 if I was forced to have sex with my husband.

Huh!

That's liberating!

I also learned that I had very strong grounds to file for divorce and annulment!

Wonderful!

The thought of freedom was finally within my reach. It was a long process, but I would do it to keep my sanity.

I was faced with the hardest battle: the father had my four aces, my children. He said he wouldn't give them unless he traveled to the U.S. with them. I just wanted my kids, not him!

My dilemma: keep fighting for my kids, or let the father keep them.

I knew deep in my heart that I didn't want to see his face anymore. Just to imagine the tip of his hair made me puke. There was too much hatred stamped in my chest for this person! The devil stirred the pot in my head.

Can I just let him keep the kids and see if he can manage to provide for them?

I could just tell him, "If you want them, then they're yours. I can have a great life here and start fresh with my man. If that's what you want, then go for it!"

But no!

That wouldn't have made me happy. That would haunt me every single minute of my life—me living a convenient life while my kids are in the Philippines? No way!

What school will they go to?

Who will take care of them?

The father?

No!

I don't want my children to see him bang different women in the house.

But maybe I can send them money, and they can still have a good life. They can go to the elite schools in the Philippines. I can provide for them.

The whole situation was mind-blowing! Coming up with the right move wasn't easy for me, but I needed to decide what was best for my children.

This war is over, dude! I will do everything for my children.

I meant it when I said it was over, but he made it very complicated. He blackmailed me by refusing to sign the children's travel permit unless he was going with them. He demanded that I also petition him. He got it. I applied for a loan to get airline tickets for all five of them.

Finally, we came to an agreement. They arrived on December 12, 2004, a little over a year after I arrived in Virginia. I spent days getting their things ready. After all the fighting, cursing, and yelling, I would finally be with them. Meanwhile, I also spent 10 of my most bitter minutes saying goodbye to my funny guy. He was letting me go and asked me to give my family a second chance. He wouldn't let me choose him over my family.

He said, "Ayos na sa akin na magmahal kahit minsan at malaman ko na minahal din ako. Nag-iisa lang ako, at nabuhay na ako ng matagal na nag-iisa. Hindi mo gugustuhin na ipagpalit ang isang buhay sa apat mong anak dahil mas importante sila. Pero wag mo kakalimutan na andito pa rin ako kahit na anong mangyari. Salamat sa pagmamahal."

(*"It was good enough for me to know how to love for once and be loved by you. I am just one person, and I have lived by myself for a long time. You wouldn't want to trade this one life with the lives of your four children because they are more important. But know that I would always be here for you no matter what. Thank you for the love."*)

And with that, we parted.

What do I do?

Choose my own happiness over my children? No, that is selfish.

Yes, it was the most difficult decision of my life, but I have always vowed to do everything for my children. It was very tempting to just go on with my life and enjoy my newfound happiness after all that I went through in life, but I knew it was the devil working. As a mother, I needed to put my own personal feelings aside and face the reality, which is to give up and sacrifice more for their sake. Mario and I chose what was right over convenience.

It wasn't easy.

While I grieved over my heartbreak, my heart leapt for joy when I saw my children walking towards Gate B at the Richmond International Airport. I drove the car Bossing gave me. I hugged them tight! Oh God, how I missed my children. The first one I checked was Belay, my youngest. She didn't look bad at all. I saw beauty sprouting off her face. Then a group hug with my little people. The father, just a side eye.

Eh!

One thing I noticed, though, was the cold hug from Audrie when they arrived. I caught her looking at me then she looked away. I couldn't read her mind. Well, it wasn't the best time to lecture and discuss things about my feud with the father. All I wanted was to savor my moment with the kids. Eventually, I found out that their father had said something bad about me—that I am a dirty woman.

The father knew about the agreed-upon rules before they arrived. We had a deal: I would bring him over with the kids, but he had to move out after six months, and six months ONLY! When that time was up, he had to find his own place. I could help him apply for a job since he was also a teacher. In fact, he was a Science Major. It may seem cruel or unfair, but he needed to learn his lesson the hard way. I had suffered enough, and it was time to end it. I needed to look and feel tough. I couldn't deal with him anymore. Not surprisingly, being the sex maniac that he is, he would even order porn movies on pay-per-view in my apartment! I saw them all in my bill. Well, I had enough of his bills back home. I let him live in my apartment for free, but porn bills? Nope! He had to pay for it.

He had his own area in our tiny apartment, but I made it clear that I was not his wife anymore; those days were over. Whenever I got the chance, I would look through his stuff. One time I saw his love notes to his classmate who was also married. His note described how he felt whenever they would see each other, but they had to be careful because her husband might find out. In other words, he was banging the *yaya* while having an affair with his classmate. This man is inexplicably shameless! I also found another thing from his stuff that was really odd: a picture of someone with a perfect body but with my face on it.

Obviously, I married a psycho!

Then we moved to a three-bedroom apartment. This move was not by choice—we were evicted. In our new place, the girls shared one room, Nique shared his room with his father, and I had my room. The deal was he would stay in his assigned room, and we would stay in ours. One night, he got into my room and started a fight. Well, I was not as naïve as I once was. Remember, I learned that I could call 911 whenever I felt threatened or thought I was in danger? We fought, wrestled, and rolled across the floor while Nique and Micci were sleeping. Audrie and Belay, in their pajamas, had woken up and were standing by the door crying as they watched the wrestling match. They begged their father to stop. That brought me memories of one of our biggest fights: the one when Nique refused to go to class because he saw me get beaten up. I needed to fight strongly this time.

I will not give up. I need to plan my moves. Where's my phone? Dang it! It's not in my pocket. Where is it? Oh, I think it's in my room. I need to win this fight this time. Uh-uh! You can't beat me now.

While wrestling in front of my two young girls, I maneuvered the fight towards the room where I left my phone. When we got into the room, I kicked him hard with all my might then closed the door! Well, I was not weak anymore. I had been eating some good food here in the U.S., and I had enough energy now. I grabbed my phone and dialed the three magic numbers. That was my very first 911 call.

Wow!

Finally, I got some help!

It felt so good!

I'm glad I'm in America now!

Since then, I have never felt scared again.

Did I make the right decision to give up my marriage?

Am I a bad person because my patience ran out?

Was I wrong to stop the violence in our relationship?

Should I let my children see us wrestle and fight regularly?

Was I ungrateful to my in-laws because I left their son after all the kindness and support that they had given me?

They will not forgive me for doing this, but their son is a total jerk!

Call me crazy if you want, but I believe I had 1,001 reasons to leave him.

My decision to end this awful relationship had undeniably hurt his family, most especially my mother-in-law. She treated me like her own child, and I love her so much. There was never a day that I felt rejected by any of them. Being a mother, she was protective of her son, but just like her, I am a mother too. I needed to protect my cubs. Having them grow up exposed to domestic violence would eventually ruin them. I made several attempts to contact his family and apologized for sticking to my decision. I know I explained to them why I did what I did. They may or may not understand my point, but one thing is for sure, I assured them that I would do the best I could for their grandchildren. I love them dearly, and I hope they forgive me. If I die right now and face my Creator, I can honestly and confidently say that I had done everything and anything to save my marriage with their family member. I remained faithful even when he wasn't. I told him once when he accused me of cheating to not worry because if I actually did find someone, I would tell him myself, and our marriage would be over. And that's what I did.

Not a fraction of this relationship can be rebuilt... sorry.

8
CHAPTER

Family Reset (Child #5 is Born!)

L ife went on. The kids were in school. Nique was in 4th grade, Micci was in 2nd, Audrie was in Kindergarten, and Belay entered Pre-K the following school year. Their father shared a roof with us for six dreadful months. The air was filled with animosity, and it just felt weird. I used to leave my laptop in the apartment, so he could apply for a job, but he ended up hacking my account. After school, the children would bang the door because nobody opened it for them.

Where was the father, you ask? Sleeping soundly!

After I found out this was happening, I gave Nique a key, so they didn't need to distract the other people in our apartment complex. I told them to unlock the door for themselves and call me to let me know they were home. It was the longest six months of my life. Now, time to move out. I'm sorry, ready or not, he had to go.

Cruel? It looks like it, but I needed to do it.

My thought was: *You are an educated person, you are not disabled, you can speak English, you are a teacher, you can drive, you are skillful, you are talented—you will be FINE! Bye!*

There were other Filipino teachers who felt sorry for him and thought I dumped him when he was still helpless. They helped him find a place to live. He shared a room with a Filipino couple, and he demanded that he spend time with his children. When someone says he cares, watch not his words but his actions. He says he loves them dearly and would call Nique constantly. But his true motive was not to check on them but to check on me. He was in my business all the time. He suspected I was seeing Mario and wanted to prove I was immoral!

He would call Mario's mom to accuse him of being a home wrecker and warned that he needed to stay away from me. Now he thinks I am important.

I don't have proof of this, but I think he called my school and told them I was an immoral teacher who was prancing around the building.

Ha!

Do I care?

Keep on, dude!

I'm up to fight now!

But he just wouldn't leave me alone.

I know I had lived an immoral life while I straightened things up. But while I was in the state of sin, I didn't fail to do my spiritual obligation to my children. My broken life pushed me more to give them the life that they deserved. When they arrived, I immediately registered all of them in religious education classes at church and had Micci receive her first communion.

While the children were settling in and adjusting to their new school, I filed for divorce. Thankfully, it didn't take long to process it. I got the Final Divorce Decree in 2005. Then he demanded an annulment.

Oh, you want an annulment?

Maybe he didn't believe in divorce because it wasn't a sacrament, or maybe he thought the annulment would get denied. So I submitted my petition. While it was in process, Mario and I got married civilly in January of 2006. At that point, I was two months pregnant with Child #5.

Pregnant again?

Yes!

I know... I know...

We celebrated our civil wedding in our apartment. Cheers!

I could not believe it, but it was true! It was so wrong, but I needed to show him that I was over it. My age (36 at that time) led to some difficulty with my pregnancy, but I still did not miss the Stations of the Cross during the Lenten Season, every Friday at 7:30 pm at St. Michael's Catholic Church. To this day, the child I carried at that time still comes to the Stations of the Cross with us. Pretty cool, right? When my ex-husband saw me with a big belly during Micci's First Communion, he backed off a little. He must have accepted that now, we were history. It was a big relief! Then, I got the annulment. Our marriage was found null and void based on the facts that the judges gathered from my petition letter and from the witnesses they interviewed about our relationship. A huge rock was pulled out of my heart when I got that letter.

That was liberating!

Talk about freedom!

While I carried Child #5, Mario dealt with one of his biggest problems: how to shelter all of us in his three-bedroom house.

Being the man that he is and taking full responsibility for all four children, he used up all of his savings and applied for a home equity to give each of them a room. He had the attic finished to make two rooms for Nique and Micci. Nothing fancy, but it was enough space to call it their own. Downstairs, he had the kitchen wall knocked down and extended the house to make a dining area and a small room for the two of us. That way, all the children occupied the rooms upstairs while we stayed on the ground floor, closer to the kitchen and laundry room. We were going to be doing a LOT of cooking and washing clothes for a while, anyway! Imagine feeding a family of seven, plus his mother (Mommy Rebecca). That was a lot, right? We stretched every dollar to give these kids the comfort they deserved.

Meanwhile, my pregnancy was a little risky because I was quite old for another baby. Aborting this pregnancy could have been my easy way out; I would have been able to avoid the shameful situation that I was faced with. But God knows I would regret it. While it was not easy, it was blissful. Mario made sure I was well-nourished and stress-free. Not a teardrop rolled down my cheek. It was my happiest and most relaxing pregnancy, unlike my four previous ones. I could just snap my fingers, and things came right up on my lap. Talk about being spoiled, huh? That's me! He would make me steak and buy me soymilk and not let me worry about anything. I was not stressed at all. But I know he was. He was loaded with a heavy responsibility on his shoulders: four growing children and a baby on the way.

The first year I didn't teach summer school was 2006. I was hibernating in our apartment while Mario's house was under construction in preparation for Cesareo's birth. I was hoping to deliver the baby on August 27th, so he and Nique would share the same birthday. I tried to push him out, but I guess he loved the good food that came down my warm belly and waited another day. Well, I was set to be induced at 7 a.m. on August 28th, but he came out normally six hours before my scheduled time. Right there in the delivery room was a confused Mario—not the funny guy this time. He didn't know what to do when I was giving birth. The nurse thought he would pass out when he heard his son's first cry. I was in my senses when I commanded him to take a picture, but his knees could barely hold his body, and his fingers were so weak that he couldn't even click the camera.

Haha!

First time dad jitters, I guess! But it didn't take long before he recovered. Looking at his baby gave him a double shot of caffeine and probably woke his senses up. With so much pride and joy, he held his baby for the first time. He was born on August 28, and was named ***Cesareo*** (in honor of Mario's dad and his noble great-great-grandfather who fought with one of our country's heroes during his time) ***Augustine*** (in honor of the Feast of St. Augustine).

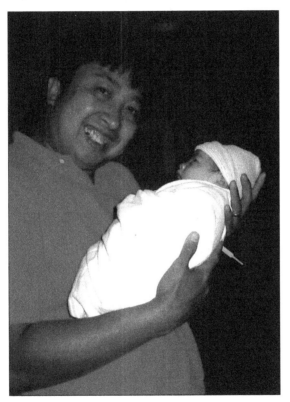

Welcome to the world, Child #5!

Thankfully, Mommy Rebecca enjoyed her last two wonderful weeks with her new grandson in Virginia because unfortunately, she passed away in the Philippines while on vacation. She didn't make it to her grandson's christening. We had scheduled it to be in April, just in time for her set arrival.

Baby Cesareo with her Mommy Becky and *Mamang.*

Then, *Mamang's* visa got approved, and she stayed with us for six years. Our hearts go out for *Mamang,* who diligently and tirelessly helped us with everything around the house. She was there for all of Audrie's basketball games, Belay's gymnastics meets, Micci's track meets, and some of Nique's football games. We couldn't have made it without her. With God's grace and abundant blessings, we managed to juggle all the challenges that came along while keeping these children alive.

After being civilly married to Mario for over a year and having the annulment approved, I could receive the Holy Communion, and I volunteered as a catechist for our church. I could also celebrate the Holy Mass without any guilt in my head.

I am free! I am free to serve my God! I am free to serve my Mother Mary! Wow!

Mario and I had our church wedding on May 11, 2008, immediately after the annulment approval (Thank you, Deacon Andy for officiating our Holy Matrimony!) It was on Mother's Day, and also the same day as Audrie's First Communion. It was a very simple ceremony attended by my immediate family and my cousin's family in Jersey. The "reception" immediately followed at our friend's birthday party at Goochland. Thanks to our good friends Resty and Imelda Raguindin, (Cesareo's godparents). In silence, we celebrated our wedding at their party without permission. Sorry for dipping in your occasion... haha! We knew you wouldn't mind at all.

Why spend on celebrating our union when there's already so much food at the party? Let's save our dollars for the children!

Mario's friends had no idea that he had gotten married; he didn't tell them because he didn't want to be in the limelight. He just wanted the blessings, not the celebration. According to him, that's all that matters anyway.

What's ironic is how we got married twice but somehow always forget to celebrate either anniversary. We've talked about it and concluded that what matters most is we are together. We celebrate our anniversary weekly when we get coffee on Saturdays at 7-11. Remember, that's where we went before we headed to the DMV to get my driving license. Does that count?

Three occasions in one day: Audrie's First Communion, Mother's Day,
and our Church Wedding.
Cheers to us...again!

*****

Looking back, I am grateful that I did not listen to other people's advice to undergo ligation after my fourth child. Had I done it, I wouldn't have been able to give my funny guy his ultimate present: a baby boy, which I risked at age 36. Thank God, he is beyond what I asked for! He is a talented boy and comes with a built-in humor machine. He is like an old man in a little boy's body. Of all my five kids, he is the only one that didn't wet the bed. He stopped wearing pull-up diapers before he turned two; he would get up and tell me when he needed to use the bathroom. He used his playpen only once and his highchair only for a couple of weeks. At a young age, he felt that togetherness, like sleeping in the bed with us and eating with everybody around the table was so important. He refused to be alone in his playpen and to be put away from everybody in his highchair. He used to love reading, but now, he would give up anything, even his X-Box time, to get out of reading. He doesn't want to read the Stations of the Cross but memorized the 14 Stations in five minutes. He would listen but wouldn't read. Yup! That's my weird boy!

Of the five, this kid claims to be the different one. He thinks it is weird to stick someone's nose in books to review for the test or memorize facts like his older siblings do.

Reading books?

He says, "Eh! Who does that?"

In his mind, being a student is hard enough, so why make it harder? Seriously, this tiny apple did not fall far from its tree. Mario is not a fan of school either. But when he was younger, Cesareo would always create something out of nothing, and sit outside and watch the birds, then go back in to draw. He was compelled to do something for the Filipino victims when he saw the aftermath of the strong typhoon on TV. He wrote a story after seeing the victims of the Hayan typhoon in the Philippines, after the visit of Pope Francis. I shared his "book" to his school principal, and the teachers and staff supported it. They issued a check to Red Cross in his name. He doesn't want to talk to other children. Does your child prefer going to the playground with other kids? Not my child. We used to wait in the car until the last kid left before we walked to the swing. How weird, right? Well, I own that kid.

To keep him awake during the Good Friday service, he drew a picture of Jesus at church while he comes up with creative stuff on regular days.

We clicked the "Family Reset" button. The kids wondered if Mario could just adopt them all, so we could all be Sta. Anas. He didn't pursue the process not because of the inconvenience and the associated cost, but because he thought it was just a name. He explained to one of them (I don't remember who specifically) that the minute he got involved with me, he considered them all as his own. From the day we got to know each other, he stepped up and took full charge of me and my loaded package, including my parents, sisters, relatives, and friends in the Philippines.

I cannot forget when he told me, *"Hindi natin pag-aawayan ang pera. Wala tayo nyan, pero kikitain natin yan."* (Money will never be an issue in our relationship. We may not have a lot of it, but it can be earned.) Now that Cesareo is big enough to join social media, his friends think he is the adopted one because all his siblings share a last name that is different from his. Well, we can't have everything.

God helped us figure out how to raise and clothe these children. We dressed them with yard sale clothes or hand-me-downs from different people. Belay came home one day when she was in grade school with a story. She said her friend liked her dress so much and asked her where she got it from.

She replied, "Oh! My mom got it from a yard sale."

Can I teach my child to lie?

Of course not!

I explained, "Next time someone asks you where you get your clothes, you can say, 'You know what, I actually forgot, but I can ask my mom.'"

Elegant, eh? That's not lying because I truly don't remember where I got my children's clothes from when we drove around on Saturday mornings to shop at yard sales. Honestly, I don't know! All I know is it came from one of the houses one Saturday morning.

There are no *Glorious Mysteries* without the *Sorrowful Mysteries*. This is the same with life. We appreciate the good times more after going through some pretty tough ones. To some people I know, going through a divorce is heartbreaking. In my case, separation, divorce, termination of marriage, or the end of the relationship was my major victory. It meant freedom from a bitter relationship. It was 12 long sorrowful years of pain, tears, and disappointments.

Just to set this straight, I'll say it again: I love his family. They are all great people, but the one I married was not like them at all. Before I migrated in 2003, I thought he would change. He did not; he was still unfaithful. I prayed for a teaching job, so I could raise my four children on my own, and God answered my prayer. He gave me a secure job and threw in a bonus at the end of my first year in Virginia. He gave me Mario, my Super Mario.

All my life, I was working and raising my little children but felt dead inside. I forgot what it felt like to have fun and be truly happy. The Final Divorce Decree and the annulment papers were the two pieces of documents that brought me to freedom. They took off the thorns that pierced my head, they healed all my wounds, and reset my life to happiness. Remarrying is my own version of resurrection. **I rose from my marital death**.

Praise be to God!

Alleluia! Alleluia!

9

CHAPTER

The Battle is Still On

After the divorce and annulment, there was a big fight over child support. Contrary to what he claimed about his longing to be with his children was his lack of desire to fight for custody. We fought over child support because he refused to contribute to any child-related expense. Instead, he wanted spousal support. According to his allegations, I abandoned him, and he deserved to be supported.

Do I need to make a list of reasons why I cut the cord?

We went back and forth at the courthouse over child support for quite a while. Finally, I won.

But did I really win?

Or he actually did?

I am not sure... it depends on how you look at it. Maybe I won because the court made him pay against his will. On the other hand, I think he won because the court made him pay only the bare minimum child support ($65/week for all four children).

Now, let's do the math: $65.00 divided by four (children) equals $16.25. Now, $16.25 divided by seven (days a week) is equal to $2.32 a day. How far can $2.32 for each child go? In other words, how on earth can I stretch $2.32 per child per day? Their school lunch already costs $2.75 a day.

Ha!

This thought hurts my brain!

Why worry about something I cannot control? At least I had a job, and I always taught summer school to augment our tight budget. The kids lived a simple life anyway. They knew our limitations, and we extended all our resources. I put more potatoes in the dishes I cooked to make them last longer. I counted 10 shrimps (and 10 shrimps only!) to be cut and give flavor to my vegetables. I recycled everything, even the food. I made new dishes out of leftovers. I just needed to strike my magic ladle and transform whatever food was left unnoticed. In my pot, I combine left-over pork chops, debone the rotisserie chicken from the previous week, throw in some eggs and rice to make freshly cooked fried rice. Thankfully, nobody got sick from what they ate.

My last encounter with my ex-husband was when he finally moved out of our shared apartment, six months after their arrival. Luckily, the father found a place somewhere in South Richmond. He demanded that he spend time with the kids. I had no problems with that; I thought that was great! They're his too, and he has all the right to be a parent. I drove them to his place, but he wanted me to pick them up as well. I thought it was his responsibility to bring them back to me. He claimed it was inconvenient. Well, being a parent is a combination of sacrifice and inconveniences. Maybe he found it difficult to sacrifice and handle life's inconveniences, so he got mad at me. One night after he dropped the kids off at the bus stop at the Applebee's near our house, he screamed at the top of his lungs. I was on the other side of the street. He called me names. I think he said, "Syakol." I don't even know what that means, but who cares?

I know a lot of people thought I was so mean for kicking him out of my place, especially some of the Filipino teachers who came to the US with me. They felt sorry for him and thought of me as the antagonist in this movie the whole time. I stand by my decision. I am done! I know what I am fighting for. I live for my children, not for my reputation. There was even an email sent to the Filipino community from an anonymous concerned person talking about how disgraceful I am and brought shame to all. Then, there was this very long email sent by one of the Filipino teachers that put me down and talked so badly about me.

I found out about it because somebody asked me if I was aware of the bad email that had been going around.

"About me? Can you send it to me, please?"

Seriously, she (one of the Filipino teachers who is actively involved in the Annual Filipino Festival here in Richmond, VA) had the time to compose a long letter about me. That was a lot of hate to write. I have a copy of that letter but to this day, I haven't finished reading it. Maybe I'll look into it one of these days because it's been in my file for years. I'll read it and recycle the paper after. I was also harassed a couple of times by other Filipino teachers and their spouses in different forms and in several occasions, but it's alright! I didn't care what other people thought of me. At the end of the day, I have all of my children.

The visitation and his communication with the children faded away. He moved to a different state and went on with his life. Occasionally, he would pop out and take the kids when his family members from the Philippines came for a visit. The kids think he got married but was unable to confirm it because they weren't directly informed about it. They inferred that he did because they saw a picture frame displayed in his place with a girl. These kids don't ask.

Shouldn't he at least tell the children if he did? They deserve to know, right?

His children were all actively involved in school playing different sports. Nique played football and wrestled; Micci did volleyball and track; Audrie played basketball, volleyball and track for a few years; Belay did gymnastics since she was six years old. When she was in 2nd grade, I requested that she take a break from gymnastics until she went to middle school because the gym fees were so costly. We needed money to buy food and pay for the bills instead. Meanwhile, I encouraged her to do cartwheels in our front lawn regularly to keep those muscular legs active. During winter, when she couldn't do her routine outside, we would talk to her with her head on the floor as she did handstands by the wall. We repainted our walls years after because there were handprints and footprints everywhere.

When Micci was older, she tried to add her father on Facebook, but he rejected the invitation. Micci was hurt. She just wanted to connect with her father, that's all. She was not even going to ask for money, yet he rejected her. When Audrie was applying for college, he refused to give his basic information. I only know his full name and birthday, not his current address, email, and Social Security number. We just needed his basic information for financial aid purposes. Do you think he provided?

No!

It didn't cost him a damn thing, yet he refused to give it. (Sorry, I cursed! Can't help it.)

Why?

I don't know!

I have made attempts to contact his family members and asked them to help me get the necessary information for Audrie's sake, but to no avail. So I implemented Plan B: I asked non-family members to verify that Audrie has no contact with her non-custodial parent. This is the most degrading thing that I have ever done for my children, to involve other people in our mess. But like what I promised, I will do anything and everything for my children.

But where's his heart?

Doesn't he want to contribute something for his child?

This should be instinct, right?

A daddy bear helps protect its cubs, but how about my children's father?

Lord, please help me comprehend this!

Whew! Images of him torture my head!

Do I have the right to be upset when I found out that he was going to attend Nique's college graduation at Virginia Tech in 2017? Please tell me if I was being selfish. Mario and I took care of his children and fed them well. We always grabbed every opportunity to earn extra income to support these little angels because their father's child support is not enough to keep them alive for even a day.

Did he ever come and watch them play their games?

Did he ever attend even one Parent-Teacher Conference?

Where was he when we needed extra hands to drive his children all around town to attend their school functions and games?

How about a little help with their yearly registration fees to attend faith formation classes throughout the year?

Or cover their retreat fees?

These children looked forward to attending church retreats. It hurts my pocket when all three girls signed up to attend an out-of-state retreat at the same time for a couple of days. I thought about discouraging them from going but didn't because at least they don't do drugs. But they are addicts... addicted to the Lord!

Now that two graduated and two are still in college, did he offer to help carry even one box when they moved into their dorm or apartment?

Ok, if not moving in, how about when they moved out?

How about just give your children some gas money since we provided a car for each one of them?

Alright, how about something that doesn't cost anything?

How about a short note to wish them good luck as they start a new chapter in their life?

How about a graduation card?

A Christmas card?

A birthday card?

How about pieces of advice?

They are good kids! They deserve it.

Do you have a single clue of what it takes to send all your four young children to school daily, ON TIME?

Do you know what it feels like to worry when they walk to the bus stop on a rainy day?

Or on a cold morning?

Did you know that I just pick up Audrie's umbrella at the bus stop because I don't have time to walk her out and wait for the bus with her because I still need to tend to your other children while I get ready for work?

Did you know that Mario adjusted his work schedule, so he could go home early and pick your children up from four different schools after their games?

Did you know what it feels like when you miss the bus by one second, and you have no choice but to drive them to their schools, which makes me stressed and exhausted before I even clock in?

Did you know that for many years, I went to work without combing my hair?

Did you know that for me, work is my time to relax and rest?

It's weird to say, but it's true. At school, I have time to sit when I read stories to my students, watch a video together, or work on counting around the carpet.

Do I have time for myself?

How about you?

Yes, you do! Because you don't have any obligation and responsibility, but all your children grew up fine.

You're welcome, Sir!

And now you want to see Nique graduate? Really? You have the nerve?

I cannot fully explain what came to my head, but I was so furious! I couldn't stop crying! Was I being selfish? I wouldn't mind sitting next to him if he did just one of the things that I thought he should do for his children. I thought it was disrespectful, and I couldn't stand it.

Two years later, he came to Richmond on Christmas Eve to see his children. According to him, he wanted to explain his side.

Explain what?

Why now?

After all these years?

One day before Christmas?

Explain why you didn't communicate with your children?

Explain why you didn't greet them on their birthday?

Why you started texting Micci and Audrie after how many years, but never texted Belay for any reason? Not even on her birthday?

Do you even know how old Belay is?

Oh, I think he knows because he has been waiting for Belay to turn 18. Now that she is an adult, he can stop paying $65/week (sometimes $72, it varies from time to time, but never went up to $75) for child support. Now it's down to $4.61 a week!

That is **H-I-L-A-R-I-O-U-S!**

Unbelievable!

Caution: This might give you a headache if you think about it seriously. I hope I live to be 2,000 years old to see his last payment from his arrears.

There were so many ways to connect with them and show them you cared if you really wanted to, but you didn't. But I think I know why.

He said they would meet up and have lunch. They left the house that day and boy, it ruined my holiday season. Micci explained that she went not because she missed him, but because she wanted to hear what he had to say. Belay didn't really want to go but went ahead because everyone else was going. On the other hand, Audrie didn't really care because she couldn't stay long anyway; she had work that day, so she only stayed for a few minutes and left. Meanwhile, Cesareo was stuck in the midst of all the drama and commotion in the house. He tried to eavesdrop and weigh things as he always does when it comes to *their* father issues.

Christmas of 2017 was my worst. I couldn't take it!

Why did you have to see him after all these years? He wasn't there for you guys when you needed him! With a text message, you get stirred up and would have lunch with him? Wow!

That broke me and made me distant to my children for a couple of months.

How unfair is that? I couldn't take it. I stopped cooking. I stopped talking. I stopped everything, except the flow of the tears down my chubby cheeks. It seemed endless. Very depressing! Mario tried to talk me out of it, but my ears refused to listen. I was mad... mad at those four children! The house was unusually quiet, and I stayed in the room the whole time. Nobody dared to talk. I wanted to go away. Mario drove me around as I cried over the whole situation. This is a different cry... I don't know. Not a hurting cry, but like a betrayed cry. I felt stabbed in the back by my own children.

He has been gone for a long time... and after everything that I had done for you people, YOU: **Nique, Micci, Audrie, and Belay**... *you still want to listen to him?*

They returned from their lunch. For the first time, our house was quiet and felt weird. No laughter, no talking, no teasing, no mocking... it was pure silence. Nique didn't say a word, didn't explain, and it bothered me even more. I couldn't take it! They cooked for Christmas Eve while I dealt with my own drama in my room. After a while, Micci and Belay tried to tell me that meeting him didn't really mean anything. What they told me about the meeting was still the usual stuff... him blaming me for everything with the intention of making my life difficult. In short, this whole meeting revealed his immaturity that made his own children angrier. I didn't hear anything from Audrie until she got back from work. What's worse was Nique seemed to disregard my feelings and didn't say a word to console me. Among the four, I expected to hear that from the oldest because he has the most memories of our bad marriage. He should have been the spokesperson, but he remained quiet.

That hurts!

Nique went ahead and cooked our Christmas meal.

So you don't care about what I feel now? Don't you want to know why I am all upset? Everybody said something except you. What do you have to say, boy? Maybe you think your father was right all along? Can you not defend me from your father who is taking revenge on me? Why? Because I abandoned him?

Cesareo didn't seem to understand what was really happening. He came and checked on me, gave me a hug, and then finally asked, *"That Papa that you guys always talk about sounds like a bad person, but I've never seen him. Is he my stepfather?"*

Now, that was really HILARIOUS! Poor thing, he felt alienated and tried hard to be a part of the situation.

Micci came home one weekend crying. She had received text messages from his father about how he remembers the time when they were all together at KFC, and now he sits there by himself. That confused Micci. She made attempts to reach out to him when she had a trip to Tennessee and had invited him for lunch. He turned her down. When your daughter, whom you haven't seen for many years, texts you and invites you for lunch, would you say no? I wouldn't! I would do everything to see her. Now that she will be an architect soon, he sends a message to remind her about their time together?!

What's your agenda, dude?

He was playing the victim again and trying to make her feel guilty. I will not forget how affected she was as we talked about it on the front porch, with her laying on my lap like she used to when she was a little girl. That was a precious moment and is locked in my head.

My take on this: *He was never restricted to come and see you, but he let the many opportunities to be with you slip through his hands. He was free to spend holidays and summer vacations with all of you, but he never did. It wasn't your fault, Micci.*

Over the years, we learned to handle our family drama on different levels. Sometimes I thought we got better at handling our emotions about him, but he still gets to us in a bad way.

Belay was applying to colleges and universities, and like Audrie, she needed the non-custodial parent's basic information. Well, he was consistent and firm. He still didn't give it. Micci tried to get it from him but to no avail. Also, Belay was devastated when she found out that he has made attempts to communicate with her older siblings. She has had her phone since she was 12 years old and never got a text message from her father, not even a birthday text.

You mean not even birthday cards from the Dollar Store?

It's two for $1.00, not that bad. He knows our address, so it wouldn't be that hard to reach out. I tell you; it was agonizing to see my little girl cry over a text message, but what could I do? Nothing. This isn't something I can impose on their father because it should be his instinct. If you're a parent, then loving, communicating, and caring for your children should come out naturally. Meeting other people whose marriages failed like mine made me label our case as unusual. All of them kept the communication open for their children.

Why can't we be like them?

I would tell him how the children were doing if he asked for it. Now, I realize I haven't had any form of communication with him since 2004. No text, no email, no calls, nothing. It's now 2019. He never asked me about how his kids are doing.

Did he even care?

Who knows!

But I know my daughter is hurt.

This is the essay Belay wrote when she was a senior in 2018. It was chosen to represent her school for the Harry F. Byrd Leadership Award.

<u>What event has been the most meaningful in developing your character? Explain why.</u>

Like most children affected by divorce, this event has held life-long impacts on my character. I was five years old when my father left my family, leaving me feel unwanted and unloved. For thirteen years I lived without a father and was left with an empty hole in my heart. Recently, I discovered that my father has made efforts to reach out to my siblings, but not me. This situation was difficult to understand. My other siblings spent more time with him and were able to form memories, while the only memory I have is crying in the middle of the night from watching him beat my mother. I never received a birthday greeting or a gesture of affection growing up, and now that he has decided to reach out to some family members, I am still neglected and forgotten. Feeling unloved by my own father is heartbreaking.

Through this pain, I have managed to transform his actions into values that I hold dear to my heart. This experience made me appreciate the people I have in my life more and strive to maintain a healthy relationship with each of them. I strongly value the importance of effective communication and its role in forming relationships. I refuse to make the same mistakes as my father, so I make sure I show my love and appreciation to those around me. In doing so, I hope to avoid leaving anyone feeling the way he made me feel. It is unusual to say I am grateful for his absence, but I am. From this disguised blessing, I have become a better person. I now try to live my life according to the virtues of forgiveness, sympathy, trust, and hope. Without this experience, it would have been harder to fully understand the importance of these traits and their role in living a meaningful life. I will use my empathy and determination to move beyond this experience and become a better friend, daughter, and hopefully, a future mother.

Well, it scarred her for life, but I'm glad she took it positively. What a heart-pinching essay!

Meanwhile, Audrie once told me when she was a sophomore in college that her father has texted her about his intention to visit her at Virginia Tech one day.

Why? To see how big you are now?

But Audrie warned me not to get hurt if she meets up with him if he ever followed through on it. When I asked her thoughts about this father issue, she explained...

I honestly don't care. There's no reason for me to be bitter or hold grudges against him. He is basically a stranger to me, so I would treat him like any other stranger. That means with a basic level of respect. Plus, I can't be mad because I have done just fine without him, thanks to you and Daddy. I am successful and incredibly blessed, and he has nothing to do with it. The reason that I work hard isn't to spite him or to show him how much better off I am without him. It was only ever to make you and Daddy proud. I owe you guys everything.

My jaws dropped as I looked at her. Oh, God! I have good children! Where on earth did she get that from?

I wouldn't feel that way if that happened to me.

My children are way better than me... seriously! They are not my improved version. They are way better versions of me. This is one of Audrie's essays when she was a senior in 2016 that hit me and made me rethink about the situation I am faced with their father.

<u>The lessons we take from failure can be fundamental to later success. Recount an incident or time when you experienced failure. How did it affect you, and what did you learn from the experience?</u>

It was out of my control. After my parents divorced in 2006, I barely saw my father. Though he had legal visitation rights to see me and my siblings, he rarely made an effort to see us. In essence, we lost a father, but I was too young at the time for it to have an emotionally devastating effect on me. Ironically, this failed relationship with my father positively affected me because it shaped me into the person I am.

I learned to be self-reliant. Life as a single mother, simply put, is exhausting. My mother was a kindergarten teacher, which meant she spent her day teaching inner-city children and came home to her four children. My siblings and I recognized that we had to make her life easier, and as a result, we learned how to take care of ourselves at a young age. Schoolwork was never an issue because it is understood that it was solely our responsibility. We were also trained to ask for help only when we absolutely needed it. In first grade, my mother instructed me to fill out my own forms and leave only the signature for her to sign—a practice that continues to this day. When my sisters and I were bored, we designed our own games to play. Our favorite was taking our papers at the end of the school year, rolling them into balls, and playing an intense game of paper dodge ball. Another way to use those paper balls was to pretend it was snow; we threw them up in the air and made snow angels. Of course, we made a mess knowing that it was our mess to clean. This way of living taught me initiative, creativity, and problem-solving skills. My independence continued to develop, and now I am equipped to handle difficult academic and social challenges on my own.

I also learned an essential quality of good relationship. Most of the time, we learn from the best, but in this case, I learned from the worst. Because the divorce had such little effect on me, it was clear that my father's behavior was not conducive to forming meaningful connections. From his example I learned that time well-spent with someone is critical in determining the quality of that relationship. The value of time is especially apparent to me now that two of my siblings are away at college. When they return home, I make the conscious decision to spend time with them. Furthermore, with this being my last year before leaving for college, I maximize my time with my family at home by prioritizing family trips, supporting my siblings at their games and meets, and planning other activities with them.

Lastly, I learned the value of commitment. Ultimately, my relationship with my father failed because there was no commitment—neither side was willing to exert the effort or make the first move. Now I devote myself to the activities and people that I am involved with because I know from experience that "you only reap what you sow." Moreover, I only take on commitments that I know I can keep. For example, I aspired to be a member of my youth group's leadership team, Teen Leadership Team (TLT). At the same time, I recognized that it was another time commitment to add on to an already busy senior year. I resolved the conflict by deciding that because I really wanted to participate, I would make time for TLT.

In some ways I am thankful for my father's actions; the situation in which he left my family taught me a lesson that I would not have been able to learn otherwise. Most importantly, I learned that it is harmful to harbor negative feelings about things beyond my control. Instead, I choose to use my father as the anti-example for building a stronger character.

I cannot disagree when people tell me that I am so blessed to have good children because it's 100% true!

*****

We all moved on and continued with our daily life. Everyone is trying to accomplish something. After Nique finished his degree in Mechanical Engineering at Virginia Tech, he joined the army. He went through basic training for 10 weeks in Ft. Jackson, NC. Then he moved to Ft. Lee, south of Virginia for more studying before flying to Eglin, Florida for his graduation. After over a year of intensive training, studying, and lots of praying, he passed all his tests and graduated as an Explosives Ordnance Disposal Specialist. Weeks before his graduation, he knew that we couldn't attend his graduation since everybody was doing something. Micci and Audrie were taking their finals for the semester, Belay was busy writing essays for her college application, and Cesareo had basketball games. In short, the timing was bad. Had he graduated in November, like he anticipated, it could have been a different story. But his paperwork and clearance took so long to process that his graduation got pushed back. It was clear to everybody that we were going to miss this important event, and Nique was aware of it too. In fact, he assured us that he would be fine when we dropped him off at the airport after his Thanksgiving visit. According to him, he will ask his old lady friend at church to take his pictures and promised to send them to me.

Friday, December 7, 2018 was when he had his nice uniform on for the first time. We were all excited for him and wished we could be there to show our support. I was so eager to ask how it went and looked forward to seeing his pictures in his fancy uniform. But since it was a school day, I tried not to get distracted and waited until after dismissal. When I got home, Mario whispered, "Did you see Nique's videos on Facebook? And do you know his father was there?" In disbelief, I dropped my bags and said, "No. I haven't checked yet." I didn't see anything in my feed, but it showed on Mario's. Only Nique is friends with his father on Facebook. Remember, he refused Micci's friend request while Audrie and Belay didn't even attempt to add him. Mario and I sat down and watched Nique's tagged videos.

What?

How did he get there?

Did Nique plan this?

Is this why he hasn't texted me and hasn't sent any pictures yet?

I did not say anything but waited all Friday night. I also watched my phone the whole day Saturday but got no text message.

Maybe he's still enjoying his father's company.

I waited all day the next day, Sunday. Still nothing from Nique. For three days, I couldn't do anything but cry. I cried a cry that was worse than my cries when I was with their father. This cry drained my brain out because I didn't know what to think. I felt *betrayed* and *disregarded* and very *disappointed* with Nique when I should be celebrating his success.

Why were you with your father?

And now you want to share your glorious moment with the person who wasn't there for you and your siblings. He wasn't there when you were growing up, Nique!

Why?

Why NIQUE?!

I watched his tagged videos over and over. I watched how his father was very proud of his only son.

Who wouldn't be?

But why was he there?

It should have been us!

I was deeply hurt. I didn't know if I could recover from this. This is the second time Nique has scarred my feelings. Was it intentional? I told the girls about it, and they too were shocked.

That weekend was unforgettable. I took pain medicine for three days to help me think clearly and to ease the pain. I felt so weak that I could hardly do anything. I shared my sentiment with my cousin (Anabel) and her husband (Gary) from New Jersey, and they felt the same way.

Why was he there?

The same question that I cannot answer... only Nique.

I could not be like this for a long time. It was already Sunday, and I hadn't heard from my soldier. That was unusual of Nique.

What is going on?

I needed to find answers and be the big girl that I thought I was. I mustered enough courage and took my phone. God helped me find a way to start a conversation. I sent him a picture of Cesareo playing in the snow.

He texted back and said, "Wow! That's a lot of snow. I graduated last Friday, and did you see Papa? I should have told you."

I replied, "You didn't tell me anything. Is that why you were ok for us not to come?"

We went back and forth, and he explained further, "I asked him after you guys said you couldn't make it. I realized I didn't want to be alone, so I figured I'd ask him just in case he could. Logistically, it was expensive for all of you to come down and the timing was terrible, so I get it. But it doesn't suck any less to be able to share it with anybody."

In my head and in my heart, I screamed, *I'd rather be alone than with that jerk who was never there when I needed him!*

But I am not Nique, and Nique is not me. He has relations with his father.

Still, I questioned him and said, "If you can make him attend your graduation, why can't you get his basic information for Audrie and Belay's college application? What's worse is when I ask people to testify that we can't provide the non-custodial parent information because you have lost contact with him, but they see you in videos hanging out with your father. What does that make me, then? A liar?"

I felt distant with my Child #1 for a year. I was in a very difficult situation. I needed help. I needed to figure out how to ease the pain. I asked God to help me because I couldn't do this alone. Mario tried to explain how this is also difficult for Nique. He is placed in the middle of it all. Mario, the most logical and rational human being in our household, stated that Nique has good intentions. He saved us some money.

Mario said, "Do you know how much it will cost if we all fly, sit there, and fly right back after an hour? Imagine the amount of money that we could have spent for this occasion. I know it is an important event, but missing it doesn't mean we love him less."

Alright, he made a point, but why did he need to invite him?

Mario explained further, "*Kahit na ano pa ang sabihin mo, tatay sya ng mga anak mo, at may karapatan sila na makita sya.*" (No matter what you say, he is still the father of your children, and they have all the right to see him if they want to.)

But how unfair is that?

We were there for all his children 24/7, but he was nowhere to be found when we needed him.

Now that it's time for glory, he shows up?

Mario added, "*Di ba yan naman ang dapat gawin ng magulang? Ibigay ang kailangan nila? Eh ang dami mo na ngang binigay sa mga anak mo, bakit ngayon ka pa titigil? Wag ka nang magtanong ng magtanong. Oo nga, hindi patas ang sitwasyon. Oo nasaktan ka, oo masama loob mo, pero hindi yun importante. Sya pa rin ang tatay, kahit na ano sabihin mo, sya ang tatay. Pero nga, pinalaki mo sila ng maayos, at hindi sila marunong magtanim ng sama ng loob na katulad mo. Hangang-hanga nga ako dyan sa mga anak mo eh! Dahil kung ako, hindi ko gagawin yun! Pero di ba yun ang gusto mong mang-yari? Mas maging mabuting tao sila kaysa sa iyo? At lumaki silang mabub-uting tao dahil sayo. Hindi ka ba masaya na mabait yang mga anak mo? Sabi nga ni Audrie, madami syang blessings na natanggap kaya wala syang lugar sa puso nya na magtago ng galit. Kung ang turing nila sa tatay nila ay stranger, at sabi ng Diyos be nice to strangers, so yun ang ginagawa nila. Talagang mas mabubuting tao yang mga batang yan, di katulad natin, kaya dapat mo silang ipagmalaki.*"

Translation: But that's what parents do, right? You provide for them. You have given a lot to your children, so why stop now? Just keep on giving. Stop questioning. Yes, it was unfair, yes, you're hurt, yes, you're upset, but that's not important. He is still their father no matter what happens. You raised them to be great kids, and they hold no grudge to him. I really admire your kids because I wouldn't do that if I were in their shoes. Isn't that what you want for your children? To be a better version of you? They are, and that is because of you. Aren't you glad they are extraordinary people? Like what Audrie said, God has blessed her with so many things that she has no space in her heart to hold a grudge. Their father is basically a stranger, and God said we should be nice to strangers. They are just being nice to a stranger. They are way better than us, a way better version of you, and that's something you should be very proud of.

Furthermore, he added, *"May special connection si Nique sa tatay nya, at di mo pwedeng ipagkait yun. Wag mo na isipin yang nararamdaman mo. Katulad ng ginawa mo dati, nagsakripisyo ka para sa kanila, eh di gawin mo ulit para sa kanila. Ibuhos mo na lang lahat sa akin yang sama ng loob mo, pero wag mo na hayaan si Nique na isipin pa yang sama ng loob mo. Masyadong delikado ang trabaho nya. Ayaw mo syang ma-distract habang nasa trabaho dahil konting pagkakamali lang, masisira sya, or baka may mangyaring masama sa kanya, and I'm sure ayaw mong mangyari sa kanya yun. Kaya, hala! Tigilan na yang sama ng loob at i-celebrate mo na yung achievements ng anak mo."*

Translation: Nique has a special connection with his father, and you can't take that away from him. Put your feelings aside, like you always did, and sacrifice again for them. You have done it before, you can surely do some more for their sake. You can just pour your heart out on me, and I will listen. I'll take all your sentiments, but don't let Nique worry about your hurts anymore. He has a very dangerous job. You don't want him to be distracted while he's doing his job because his work is very risky. Let him focus and not worry about anything. A small error might mean trouble in his nature of work. He can get seriously hurt, and that's something you don't want to happen. So get your act together, and just celebrate your child's achievement.

I let that thought sit in my head for a minute, then I called Cesareo to watch his brother's video for the first time. After watching and with teary eyes, he wondered why his Kuya Nique didn't invite us. I assured him that he did, but we couldn't go because everyone was busy, so he invited his father instead. He sat there quietly while looking at his brother's pictures with admiration, then he turned to me and said, "Mama, you cannot tell Kuya Nique who NOT to love. His father sounds like a bad person, but he gave my siblings the gift of life. If not for him, I wouldn't have any brother or sisters, and that would be very sad."

Then, tears rolled down his cheeks.

That grabbed me by the heart! You must have a stone heart if that did not move you at all. He is a 12-year-old boy but can dig deeper and see what is unseen by most adults. I choked and remained speechless for a few minutes. I looked at him and thanked him for giving me the Christmas Miracle that I have been praying for. I had a flat tire for a while, but I fixed it with Divine Intervention. God does work in mysterious ways. The Holy Spirit came down on him and spoke God's words.

The first time we were not there for you.... sorry. But you made us all very proud, Kuya Nique!

Hey, Lord! You definitely gave me great kids! Thank you!

It gives me chills as I write this part. Christmas 2018 was when I felt I was healed. Now, all about their father is just a laughing matter. I realized that I was so affected by it, and I let it control me over the years. I learned to let go and change my perspective which made me a lot happier than ever before.

Thank you, my little Cesareo!

Life is not perfect and is unfair. I'm sorry, we are a divided family. I wish this issue did not exist, but it is through challenges that we learn life's lessons. Cesareo was right, his life will never be as happy as it is now if not for his siblings. Ok, I will bend down and look at things differently for my children. I shouldn't be bothered by anything about their father. I volunteered to be a Eucharistic Minister, and I am not worthy to give out the precious Body and Blood of Jesus if I can't give my peace to their father. It is hard to be me, I don't even want to be me sometimes, but I would do this for me, my children, and for the Lord. I will offer this journey of healing to God and my Mother Mary.

I am willing to make peace with him, and I look forward to the day when I can look at him eye to eye and say, "I forgive you even though you never asked for forgiveness."

The one good thing about our family drama is the father didn't fight for custody. My children have been with me, and they have always been there for each other as they went through their childhood issues, school problems, and even boy problems. They literally grew up together, learned from each other, and shared whatever is available for them. They didn't feel the emptiness or felt neglected at all because we patched each other's holes. It wasn't easy to be available to all these five children with different needs, but we survived it all. God made it all work for us!

I fought my battles against the "Goliaths" of my world and won them all with my slingshot of faith and prayer.

Thank you, Lord, for keeping me strong!

The five reasons why my heart grows bigger each day.

10
CHAPTER

We Made It!

I won't mind whatever life throws at me, at least I have five happy children.

I blinked a few times, and now they're grown. Life is a mystery. I still can't believe how Mario and I managed to raise these five kids. We lived by the day. Conceiving them when I wasn't ready was a sorrowful event, but watching them turn out the way they have is such a glorious sight. I had the choice and could have aborted them, but God intervened. I'm glad I didn't because guilt would have been my worst enemy. Without a doubt, and I want to say this again, I have great kids! We hustled our way to the top and made it with God's help.

I can't stop smiling when people say I am blessed and wonderfully favored with phenomenal children because God not only molded them beautifully, but He also gave them smart brains and wired them for success in their own fields. They are all talented in their own way. Maybe they're not the best athletes on their team, but they worked very hard to be an asset in whatever sport they're in. I commend them for the way they perceive things and how they share what they think about issues concerning life, friends, family, education, relationships, and the state of the world. Sometimes, Mario and I catch ourselves just looking at them with admiration when they say things that we would never have thought of. The tables have turned; they teach *us* life lessons now. In our household, there is no stepfather and no half-brother. We are one family, and we are a great team. I was surprised at how they gradually changed the way they call Mario. I introduced Mario to them as *Tito* (Uncle), but as they grew more comfortable with him, they eventually transitioned to calling him "Daddy" and "Darling." I had no influence over this. It was entirely up to them. I never required them to call him a certain way, but they did at their own time, which I think is great.

Since they are all actively involved in different sports, we set the rule early on. We will watch their games until the end of middle school. Once they are in high school, e.g. once we start having to pay to watch their games, we will just give our blessings as we pray for sendoff.

"I love you, good luck! Be safe, and see you at home."

What, you think we should have paid and sat there for hours? Well, not for every game! I could have used the admission money to fix dinner for our family. Now let's do the math... again: it costs $36 ($6 x 6) for the whole family to watch one game for one child. $36 for the child who plays gymnastics and another $36 for the other child who plays football. Another $36 for the one who plays volleyball, and another $36 for the one who plays basketball. They compete every week!

Do you realize how many 25 lb. bags of rice I can buy with all that money?

I just told them, "Don't forget to pray before game time! May God protect you and keep you safe, but I'll have a nice dinner for you when you get home."

As expected, they are really hungry after practice or games. They always looked forward to a sumptuous meal and couldn't wait to go home, so they would race to the door, sniff, and guess what Asian cooking was steaming out of the big pot. Actually, they are always hungry. You can leave cash or pieces of jewelry on the countertop and expect it to be untouched, but not with food—food goes really fast. Label anything that is not meant for sharing, put a note, sign the container, or hide it in the refrigerator by the laundry room. My children are food monsters!

My children don't fight; I never saw them fight and scream at each other like what we normally see in the movies. The only time that they butt heads is when it comes to issues concerning food. Every now and then, we would decide to go out to a restaurant as a family. This sounds pleasant, but it often caused problems because they all have to agree on a place to pick. Recognizing that this is a special occasion, they would sit around and put all their brains out. It's so funny to see how they exchange each other's preferences, and the oldest child "does the research" before presenting the options to the team. I am not kidding! This is a serious family matter. They feel the need to pick the right food, the right place, and the right price because this is a rare treat. Now that they're grown, the birthday kid picks the place, but one rule is still in effect: no soda!

Do the math again... if everybody orders a soda or an iced tea, that's almost $20 on top of the bill.

"No! Drink your soda in the car! I have a cooler in the van and have a variety of drinks to choose from. You can have as much as you want from that."

Later on, Mario and I started to let loose a little bit. We set aside a weekly budget for eating out after the Sunday mass. It was just to give them a break from eating my home-cooked meals and also gave us a chance to enjoy each other before they all grew up. We tried to eat out regularly just to savor the grace of God around the table. It didn't have to be fancy, but at least we had time to sit and talk, talk and mock, mock and tease each other, just being the weird Asian family that we always are. We just wanted to maximize our family time every weekend before the first child left for college.

We always went to the 9:15 a.m. Sunday mass and sat at the front pew right behind the crucifix. I picked that spot on purpose. I wanted them really close to Jesus even when we were at church, so they could keep their eyes on Him and not fall asleep while our priest was giving the homily. Also, they had to be on their best behavior because that's where the ambo is (where the Liturgy of the Word is read), and everybody is looking in that direction. You know, being Catholics, we sit, stand, sit, kneel, sit, stand, and kneel (we remain standing at St. Michael's when we know it's time to kneel at other churches). When we are all standing, I look to spot check what they are wearing and admire how they fixed themselves. I look once, twice, and mumble to myself, *"Oh, God, I have so many kids!"* Sometimes, I still can't believe it. It's difficult to fathom, but it's true. They're all mine.

When we would go to a buffet restaurant when they were younger, and they would be asked for their age, they knew the drill; they were seven years old and even slouched back to make themselves look shorter.

It worked!

Did they ever complain about this tacky parenting?

Nope!

I think they were fine with it because they enjoyed the family bonding more than the fancy food.

In spite of all the "father issue" drama that we were dealing with when they were young, Mario and I focused on building happy memories as a family. We went camping and purchased a timeshare, so we can visit different places on a tight budget. The most expensive trip we had was when we went to Disney World in Florida. Nique came home from college for winter break. We took advantage of the time while they were all available, and Cesareo was big enough to remember this once-in-a-lifetime event. We maximized our time and visited all the princesses.

Guess who cried when she met Cinderella?

I don't know what happened to me, but I couldn't stop the tears of joy! It was so magical! It must have been a dream come true for me since I had a deprived childhood, and Cinderella is the only Disney story that I had seen (from other people's TV) when I was little.

My children looked at me in disbelief and asked each other, "Why is mama crying?"

Then we needed to give up the timeshare because they were all growing up and not everyone was always available to go on a family vacation. Also, we felt that the monthly payments for all these timeshares needed to go to their college education instead. Cesareo was the most devastated when we finally gave up the timeshare. But we still went to places with whoever was available to keep the family bonding going. We would go to a drive-in-the-ater or just drive to Virginia Beach to enjoy the fierce waves or drive up to the Shenandoah Valley to hike and enjoy the waterfalls in the mountains. The family van, our dependable companion and witness to all the fun family trips, is still up and running.

On regular weekends, when the weather was nice, we would set up tents in the backyard, throw something on the grill, light up the fire pit, and just enjoy a movie outside. We painted the deck together and jammed to our family song, *September* by Earth Wind and Fire. We raked the leaves together, decorated the house together, and even planted together in the spring. There are just too many fun memories embedded in and around the house. We enjoyed each one of them when they were young. Now that Cesareo is big enough to recognize his many blessings, he appreciates everything and values our humble home. I say our home is built with love, painted with faith, and extended with trust.

Our house is our little church. This is where they witnessed, heard, and felt the love of God. We made God tangible in each other. We went through our joyful and sorrowful experiences and are now reaping the glorious fruits of our togetherness. It is in this house that we shelter our little disciples of Jesus. In our humble home, Mary and an angel greets you as you enter the door. When you look around, you will see a crucifix or a cross above every door. You go to the tool shed and there, you will meet the Sacred Heart of Jesus. And in the laundry room, you will see a tiny cross. If you're out in the backyard, you will see garden rocks with religious sayings. And when you go upstairs, there's Mama Mary with open arms saying, "Welcome home." You can't help but hold her hand, a simple gesture to say, "Thank you." As you take your keys before you leave the house, there is the little wall statue of Our Lady of Lourdes, a gift from my cousin Anabel when she went to Portugal, wishing you to have a safe trip and praying that God may represent you wherever you go. If you go to our house, there's no way you'll miss God because He is just everywhere!

I wasn't surprised when one of Audrie's friends once said, "There's so many *Jesuses* in your house!"

Well, for a big family like ours, we need a lot of Jesus. By the way, we have an extra Jesus in the backyard, and by the mailbox for the mailman and for those who live in our neighborhood. There's Jesus for everybody!

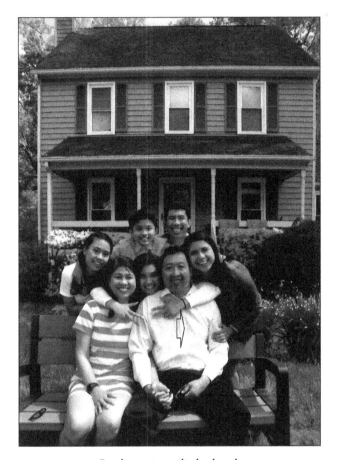

Our house is our little church.

We signed up to do different religious obligations. Now we go to different mass times. The girls attended the 5 p.m. mass on Sundays until they graduated from high school while I still attend the 9:15 a.m. masses with Cesareo and Mario to teach the Children's Liturgy. Nique, as promised, still went to church when he was in college and still goes even now that he is in the army. This is something I made clear to all my children. I give them the blessing to go out and party all night, but they need to devote an hour a week for the Lord.

"Please don't forget to do your Sunday obligation. Go to mass. I will not be there to monitor your actions, but you know, SOMEBODY does."

A teacher's pay and a regular office manager's salary can only go so far for five children, with two of them in college at the same time. But God is so good that He knows what we need even before we ask for it. Nique, who was not a citizen at the time he was applying for colleges, didn't qualify for big scholarships and grants. So Mario put the house on equity to help cover his college expenses. Time flew by very quickly and my chunky boy finished with a degree in Mechanical Engineering at Virginia Tech. He recently got married and enjoying his new phase in life. Micci, the baby girl I thought I would lose, received some scholarships, grants, and financial aid and was actively involved in her school. She was sent to India to do research and unexpectedly, her work was published in the Studio Prize Magazine. She finished a degree in Architecture at University of Virginia. She was hired to work in an architecture firm in Manassas, Virginia two weeks after her graduation. Meanwhile, Audrie was a recipient of the Knights of Columbus scholarship from our church and has received lots of scholarships from different institutions which covered most of her education costs. She gets internship opportunities from different big steel companies every summer. Now, she's finishing her internship in North Carolina with a special article from a Steel Industry magazine being one of the steel intern scholars. She is a junior at Virginia Tech majoring in Materials and Science Engineering with an overall 5th ranking. She still gets scholarships from different institutions. Last time I checked, she received her ninth one. Belay, the one who I used to think as the "ugly baby," is now a beauty. She attends University of Richmond with a Presidential Scholarship and University Grant that will cover most of her college education. She received three additional scholarships before her high school graduation. She will major in Accounting. Last but not the least, Cesareo is geared towards Biomedical Engineering. He is in the 8th grade and will be with us for a while.

Thank you, Lord, for these wonderful children!

Now that the fifth child is growing older and has heard and witnessed some of the drama about his siblings' father, he wondered why his last name was different.

He asked me, "Do my siblings' teachers even know I'm their brother since I'm a Sta. Ana?"

People are surprised when they find out Mario is not their biological dad. Maybe this is because he has acted like a real father to them since day one. He was a brave man to have allowed me to enter his life with four little kids. He did not expect anything in return and will never ever expect the kids to repay him. He is a joker, yet the most logical person I know. He recognizes that these children are busy growing up and making their own lives, and he will not depend on them for anything when he grows old.

His take on this is, "I will do what I can do for them, and if it wasn't enough, I apologize."

What a great man!

God has answered all my prayers and has always given me more than what I prayed for. So, who am I to whine about what the real father did to me in the past when Mario filled up all the emptiness in my life?

I said this to him as a joke: "You must be very picky to have stayed single at 46."

He replied, "Yeah, I was very picky. There's not a lot of women who have four kids, and it took me a while to find that woman!"

Yup!

Very picky indeed!

Yes, it's been 13 years of busy life. Now, we feel the empty nest. We had this tradition of praying the rosary and putting the sign of the cross with Holy Water on the forehead to whoever is up to a big change in their life. It can be leaving for college, army training, taking a big test, or starting a new internship in a different state. We bless each other. Now that they are in different places, we keep the communication lines open. We get regular calls and text messages. Also, I felt the need to get on Snapchat and Instagram to stay in their loop and keep abreast of what's going on in their lives. It's always exciting to hear them talk about their victories, their community service, newfound friends, academic achievements, and professional recognitions. They get internships here and there, and job offers from different companies.

Imagine what this mother feels like to hear her children talk about how well they're doing in their school and workplace.

What is more glorious than that?

God made me an instrument to make good children. They're not actually mine; they're God's. I give them back to God and pray that they become a blessing to other people as I was blessed to have a Darling to spend the rest of my life with.

Cesareo said, "I have such a good life! I don't want to die because life is beautiful. I wonder why people kill themselves when there's so much to do. Thank you, Mama, for working hard. I love you, Daddy, and thank you for being great parents. Now I don't need to worry about being poor because you took care of all that. You let me enjoy my life. I don't need anything because I have my family. We are not rich, and we don't have a big house, but it is full of love."

Cesareo's essay came to me as a surprise because I always thought he looked at me as a monster mom. That is, until I read the paper he wrote when he was in 7th grade.

"The Most Important Person to Me"

Without your mom, you wouldn't be alive right now. Being a mom is one of the hardest jobs in the world, especially for an immigrant that came from a different country raising 5 annoying children, including me. My mom is the most important person to me because she is loving and a real disciplinarian.

My mom never had the perfect childhood in the Philippines. It was a difficult life, but she still stayed tough to raise the best siblings that I could ever have. She eventually gained enough money to move to America to give me and my siblings a perfect life.

My mother is constantly the best person to everyone she meets. She always thinks the positive way out. She is the best mom for me and my siblings, the best teacher for her students, and the best wife to my hardworking

Dad. She might not be able to help me in Math but can still give me a hug when I need it.

This is why my mom is the most important person in my life. I also learned that no matter how much you hate your parents, they will still love you back.

To him, it is not special without any of these family members.

*****

Timing is everything, and everything is timing in love and loss. The Heavens heard me when I went for a walk that one gloomy night and looked at the stars. I knew deep down in my heart that one star was meant for me. The universe worked its magic and helped Mario and I find each other.

What are the odds?

He lived in Marikina, close to where I lived in Manggahan, Pasig. We might have been in the same jeepney at one point, but it wasn't time for us to get to know each other yet. He left the Philippines in 1993, the year I got married. I applied to teach in California and Nevada but ended up in Virginia. When I was in Virginia, we never met until that one night after

Hurricane Katrina, after we lost our power. We never met at any Filipino parties that I went to. God turned my life upside down in 10 minutes. It's hard to explain but seems like the balance of power shifted in our favor.

Remember my most magical 10 minutes?

It's been 16 years since the first time we met, and things have been great. Life is not long enough if you have found the right one. I fear regret more than I fear failure. You never know if things will work out according to your plan, but at least I tried. Looking back, I'm glad I gave myself a second chance and would not trade anything for millions. Having the great kids that we raised together and sharing the simple life that is left for us feels like winning the mega millions lottery. What else can I ask for when God has given me everything that I need? We have a beautiful family, and that's all that I prayed for. Everything about us is not fate but rather God's will. We vowed to commit when the father of my four kids quit.

This year is a milestone for both of us. Mario just turned 60, and I turned 50 this summer of 2019. We are soul mates. We enjoy every little thing. Who else gets coffee from 7-11 or Wawa every Saturday? And why not treat ourselves at Starbucks? But only on PROMO days: buy-one-get-one day. Who else saves every coupon at grocery stores and registers for free meals from different fast food chains? Who else has apps for all the free stuff and discounts? Who else goes on a Fri-Date Night to enjoy a $ollarita ($1 margarita) and half-priced appetizers at Applebee's? Who else stays in the car and comes up with a cleverly cheap plan? The $ollarita promo ends at 9 p.m. while the half-off for appetizers begins at 9 p.m. Again, timing is everything, and everything is timing. We check in at 8:45, order our drinks, and wait for 9 p.m. to get our appetizers.

Smart, eh!

I love going out with my cheap date.

All our money went to the kids, but we never fought about anything, especially money. I don't pay the bills. I swipe the credit cards. He warns me to watch out for smoke when I swipe a card. When I see it burning, that means give it a break. Stop using it. Use the other one. I don't know how he juggles our funds, but he does a good job.

After I realized I didn't have a little kid anymore, I felt a new kind of freedom. Now, I can do whatever I want. Now, I do Zumba (when I feel like it), do my karaoke with my Pop Solo microphone, cook whatever I feel like eating, record as many shows as I can, and binge watch all the movies available on Hulu, Netflix or Amazon.

My problem now is what to eat while I watch my movies. Life is just so good that I have too many options. It's overwhelming and can be confusing. I started drinking margaritas at age 46, when Child #1 worked as a bartender and learned to mix drinks. He let me try, and I loved it!

I got tired of crying about Marriage #1 while I laughed nonstop with Mario. I am at my best with Darling. He helped me rediscover myself and gave me his unconditional love day and night.

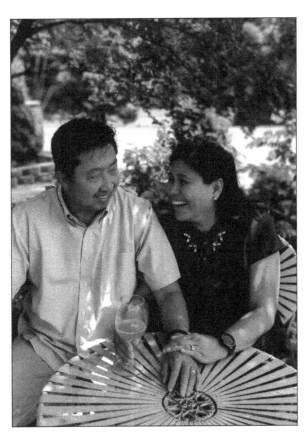

Meet my funny guy!

We don't need anything else but good health and each other. We just want to spend more time helping at church and pray for the children's safety and success. Darling is my savior and hero. My Super Mario is my superhero who never fails to say "I love you and thank you" every single day. He loves me too much, and it can be overwhelming.

Whew!

God really answers all prayers...I mean all my prayers. He gave me someone like Mario. He could be overwhelming that sometimes I say, "If you say 'I Love You' one more time, I will be upset with you. I know you love me, and you don't have to say it over and over."

Now, I am the bad person here.

Don't forget God when you get what you prayed for.

I don't. I thank Him every day.

I am very thankful for my Bossing!

He changed my life as I changed his. He takes care of me and unselfishly gives whatever I ask for — what else is more glorious than that? With great kids, a stable job, great friends, fun co-workers, nice neighbors, a great church, and...I can buy shoes and clothes when I want and don't have to wait until Christmas. Now, I can buy Starbucks coffee every day but choose not to. I can make my own coffee and buy a variety of creamers. We can eat out if we want to but would rather cook my own food in my newly renovated kitchen (my new kitchen is my lifetime all-occasion gift: Mother's Day, birthday, Christmas, and Valentine's Day). While his siblings used their inheritance money to buy brand new cars or spend it as a down payment to purchase a new house, his share went to remodeling my kitchen.

Who wouldn't love a selfless man like Darling?

Most of all, God gave me a wonderful family with five great children.

We are glad we have Cesareo, our big baby, who makes us laugh all the time. He thinks he can be a Deacon because he knows he can be naturally funny. He gets everything that he asks for. If he asks for a Sonic Hotdog, Five Guys hamburger, or a Subway Footlong, he gets it. He has a smart phone and an X-Box, which he inherited from Nique. He doesn't ask for anything extraordinary, but he is the only privileged kid to enjoy these little "luxuries" in life.

And every time he gets what he wants, I look him in the eye and say, "Cesareo, you are one lucky kid. I never had that when I was your age." I probably sounded like a broken record, so in defense he would reply, "Mama, you always say that. I'm sorry, but it's really not my fault you were poor before."

I glared at him, but he's actually right. He has nothing to do with my economic condition in the past, and why does he need to take the blame? He can be very funny while also making so much sense. We gang up against this little guy all the time knowing that he has the most comfortable life in our house. He grew up having everything that he needed and gets all the love from every family member. He was never hungry and never had to sacrifice his time to look out for any younger siblings, unlike the other four. That's how we painted his life in our head until we read the essay he wrote in his English class in October of 2018.

The Only Child

Next year I will be an only child because my sister is going to college, and I will be the only one in the house. I remember when all 4 of my siblings were still in the house, and we would always do everything together. Everything was fine until they all went to college. The house started to get quiet and quiet. I will miss the noise and the sounds around the house. So next year, I will surround myself with friends to help fill the void of being lonely.

Now I am just thinking about all the problems I will have in the future like Math and all my other subjects. It was all fine until my big brother left to college which was the first wave. I remember crying because he wasn't coming anytime soon. Then the second wave, when my other sister left, but I didn't really care about that wave. Then I realized everyone is leaving, and soon enough I would be all alone. Then the third wave, my favorite sister, Ate Audrie left, and then it was just me and Ate Belay, the last two. So next year I am preparing for the fourth wave, the final wave. I will try to do camps and after school activities to help me and to keep myself occupied when I am alone in the house.

I will overcome this challenge in my life by making friends. That way, they can help me with things when I cannot get help from home. My dad's friends are like a second family to me, so I can hang out with them when I am feeling sad. I plan on trying out this year for basketball. Hopefully, I make it, so I have something to look forward to this year. Eventually, I will get through these challenges physically and mentally.

Cesareo's four waves: His life will never be the same without his sibs.

*****

With reflection and careful thought, I had a conversation with my inner self. It was December 11, 2018 when I made a note to myself: *I don't want to cry about their father issues anymore.* I will stop questioning how he is as a parent to my children. Rather, I'll focus on what else I can do for them. I will keep doing the best I can, and that's all that matters. At the end of this life, I will look back before I breathe my last and whisper to all of them, **"I did the best I could for all of you."** And I wish that it's what they will put on my tombstone. As I said before, I volunteered to be a Eucharistic Minister, but I don't think I have earned the right to distribute the Body and Blood of Jesus to others when I am not at peace with myself. That's not what God wants from me. He wants me to be better for Him. My children are not a part of my feud with their father, and they have all the right to be with him. It is me who is the real problem. I was selfish! God just answered my prayer, he cleared my chest.

Why worry about something I cannot change nor control? Instead, I will change the way I look at things. Perspective makes all the difference!

The decisions that we make in life will define our legacy when we are gone, and this is the legacy that I want to leave behind.

December 28, 2018 at 1:15 p.m. was when Nique and I finally talked about his father. We honestly felt sorry for him, and we recognized that it is indeed very sad to be alone on Thanksgiving Day, Christmas, and New Year. But he did that to himself. He allowed it to happen. I admit that I am not triggered as much anymore about their father issues after I read Cesareo's feelings about his life being miserable without his siblings. It hit not just my heart but my soul. This kid says the funniest and the most heart-wrenching words. It was the Christmas miracle that I was praying for. Audrie's take on this: "The Holy Spirit came down on Cesareo."

I agree.

From now on...

I will TRY hard not allow his presence to trigger me.

I will not ask why he wasn't there for my children.

I will not ask why he didn't support my children.

I will not ask why he refused to be a part of their lives.

I will not ask why he hasn't apologized to what he did to me.

I will not wonder why he never thanked me for raising his children.

I will not ask why he never greeted my Belay a Happy Birthday.

I will never ask why he shows up only when it's convenient for him.

I will never wonder if he was at least thankful to Bossing for stepping up and embracing his children like his own.

Never again will I ever question anything about him because God has answered all my queries and has put my life in order. I have forgiven their father because God commands us to forgive and love unconditionally, anyway. I decided to do this because I love God, and I want to obey Him. Forgiveness has also set me free.

I mentioned earlier that we sit around and pray the rosary (not daily but it should be) when something big is coming up like one is going to college, one is having a big test, project, job hunting, deciding which school to go to, or on New Year's Eve to welcome the brand new year. Mario and I used to take turns to lead the prayer, and slowly delegated the work to the children. They take turns to lead each decade of the rosary. After doing it for a while, the first rosary in 2019 shook me and made me think, *my five children are the mysteries of my life*! I went through my *Sorrowful Mysteries* fighting my battles from a bad marriage while I raised them, but it was all worth it because they gave me the *Joyful Mysteries* and inspired me not to give up despite all the challenges. Now that we've crossed the bridge together, they became my *Glorious Mysteries* not just to our household but to everyone with whom they work with in different places.

What an amazing sight to see them prosper in their own fields and still maintain a good character with deep set faith in God.

They wouldn't turn out this way if not for the people who inspired, challenged, and taught them everything that they know. I thank their teachers, friends, our Filipino community who became our extended family and supported them, and our St. Michael's parish, especially Fr. Dan, Elise Chapman, Mike and Taylor Horvath, Patti Kamper, and their catechists from Pre-K to high school. The world around them can be cruel and unjust, but because they were always surrounded by good people, they stayed strong.

You know who you are, and I thank you from the bottom of my heart.

Salamat po ng marami!

Meet my crazy weird Asian Family.

Epilogue

I believe that everything that happens to us has a reason. Since I was the third child, *Mamang* told me that *Papang* forced her to abort me because they were financially unable to support another kid. As I remember clearly, *Mamang* narrated that she was six months pregnant with me when *Papang* squeezed a tablet in her mouth, but she hid it and spit it out when he wasn't looking. Also, he would "kick" her stomach, so *Mamang* would bleed. Now that explains why I have this flat and gigantic nose, as you see on the book cover! It was pushed back while I was in my mother's womb. Haha!

I survived it though, and I came out of this world. I took that thought to my heart and pledged to be a good person, to glorify God for protecting me when I was too helpless to save my own life. Now that I'm grown, I want to prove to my parents that I wasn't a mistake and can be one of their good contributions to humanity. I am determined to make them proud. I am here to serve my God. I discovered my purpose: to become a mother, a wife, a teacher, a sibling, a good person to my new acquaintances, and to be your friend.

Along the way, my sad and painful experiences shaped me to be the person that I am today. If God brings it to me, He will help me get through it. He didn't let go of me when I was about to break. He gave me a sense of direction.

Writing this book made me whole again. It helped me process things. I dug the pain out of my chest and opened my life to all of you. While this book describes the sorrowful, joyful, and glorious moments of my life. It serves as my personal therapy because it cleared out all my pains, tears, and heartaches from the past.

It healed all my open wounds. I still cry not because I'm bitter or hurt, but because I am thankful that I have resurrected from my own version of death. Now, I live my present with joy in my heart, have forgotten and forgiven those who have wronged me, and now face my future with abundant blessings from above.

God is good, all the time! And all the time, God is good!

He ended my pains and prepared me to enjoy the fruits of my labor.

Here I am Lord, I present to you my life with Darling and my children. Use us to spread Your Word, and may we glorify Your name in everything that we do.

Now, I feel so light knowing that my sad days are over, and I just sit and watch my children blossom to be God's disciple in their own field, while I drink my coffee with Bossing, who never quit, but stayed committed since the day he held my hand in October of 2003.

I am loving the life I live and living the life I love.

God bless, and I hope *Aurora* has touched you in one way or another.

May the love of Jesus and Mary live in our hearts forever, Amen!

Maraming, maraming salamat po!

Acknowledgments:

1. **Lori Bagli and Teresa Eastep**–*They not only inspired me to write but pushed me to make this book a reality. They suggested that I write about my life after hearing bits and pieces of my story. I volunteered to help these two women take care of Belay's (Lady) Confirmation Retreat group in October of 2017, but I ended up being helped by the young crowd in front of me. I saw, heard, and felt God in each one of them that weekend.*

2. **Audrie Corral** – *My Child #3, my junior editor, who helped polish my writing. Thank you, Aud, for patiently editing even when you are busy with your life as a student/intern. I love you very much!*

3. **Grace De Manuel** – *My editor from a different continent and my newfound friend in the Philippines. She is one of God's little angels. Thank you, Grace, and I can't wait to meet you personally!*

4. **Rolly delos Santos** – *My long-time friend, consultant, and favorite artist who made the portrait of my book cover and wrote the Foreword for me. I can't thank you enough for your valuable contribution to this book. Salamat, Friend!*

5. **Mrs. Juanita Walker** – *Our Church Lady, who boosted my confidence and believed that my story needs to be published and be shared. She is my "Church Mom," and I love her dearly.*

6. **Bossing, Nique, Micci, Audrie, Belay, and Cesareo** – *who read my draft, gave me feedback, and helped me put the pictures together for this book. I love you guys more than you'll ever know.*

7. **My best friend Eppie and her whole family especially Nanay Baby**– *for embracing me and treating me as their own family member.*

8. **My college classmates and friends** – *who accepted me the way I am and never judged me. I love you, guys!*

9. **Flordeliza Cabellon** – *my new found friend who helped me meet the requirements with the images and her technical support.*

10. **To all of you my readers** – *thank you for supporting my fundraising project. Salamat po ng marami!*

CPSIA information can be obtained
at www.ICGtesting.com
Printed in the USA
FSHW020022240120

9 781630 503703